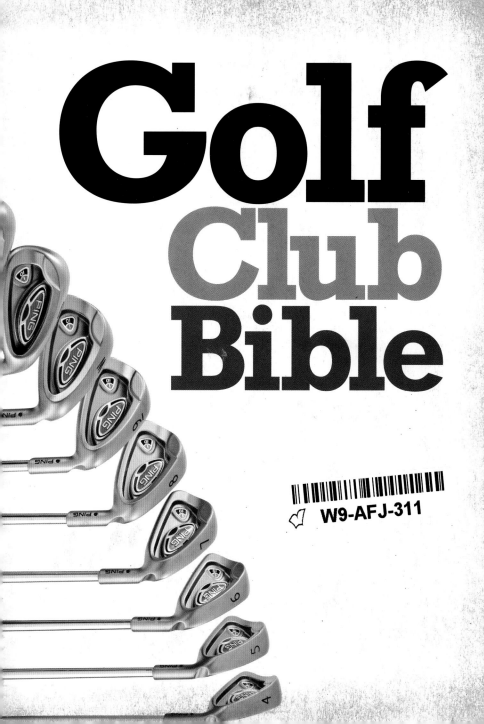

Golf
Club
Bible

A FIREFLY BOOK

Published by Firefly Books Ltd. 2009

Copyright © 2009 Marshall Editions

First printing

Publisher Cataloging-in-Publication Data (U.S.)

Pearce, Lee.
    Golf club bible : how to choose the right clubs for your game / Lee Pearce.
[192] p. : col. ill., col. photos. ; cm.
Includes bibliographical references and index.
Summary: Includes a short history of golf, a detailed explanation of each golf club, how to select and customize each club, an analysis of each swing, how to purchase clubs and a special section on ladies' clubs.
ISBN-13: 978-1-55407-495-2
ISBN-10: 1-55407-495-9
1. Golf clubs (Sporting goods). I. Title.
796.352028 dc22 GV976.P437 2009

Library and Archives Canada Cataloguing in Publication

Pearce, Lee
    Golf club bible : how to choose the right club for your game / Lee Pearce.
Includes bibliographical references and index.
ISBN-13: 978-1-55407-495-2
ISBN-10: 1-55407-495-9
    1. Golf clubs (Sporting goods). I. Title.
GV976.P42 2009 796.352028'4 C2009-902602-3

Published in the United States by
Firefly Books (U.S.) Inc.
P.O. Box 1338, Ellicott Station
Buffalo, New York 14205

Published in Canada by
Firefly Books Ltd.
66 Leek Crescent
Richmond Hill, Ontario L4B 1H1

Conceived, edited, and designed in the United Kingdom by
Marshall Editions
The Old Brewery
6 Blundell Street
London N7 9BH
www.marshalleditions.com

For Marshall Editions
Publisher: Jenni Johns
Art Director: Ivo Marloh
Managing Editor: Paul Docherty
Layout & Editorial: Seagull Design
Project Editor: Deborah Hercun
Indexer: Lisa Footitt
Production: Nikki Ingram

Originated in Hong Kong by Modern Age.
Printed and bound in China by
Midas Printing International Limited.

Lee Pearce

Golf
Club
Bible

How to choose the right
club for your game

FIREFLY BOOKS

Contents

Introduction

Although the Alliss family have been involved in the world of golf for nigh on 100 years, there are still parts of the game that fascinate me. Golf hasn't really changed since it's conception, but there is an endless flow of words and deeds that forever provides an ongoing mass of information, ideas, theories and dreams, all adding up to a wondrous part of the game itself.

I am continually astounded that golfers find themselves in ever newly created situations during a simple round of golf! The Rules of the game, which started off written on one page, now consist of a volume comparable to the *Encyclopedia Britannica*, and yet every year situations arise calling for new rulings and explanations. Over the years, hundreds of books have been written about the game and its players and how it was spread around the world, whether by Scottish engineers bound for South America or India (who for some reason took along their golf clubs) or by members of the diplomatic corps, who were trying to spread the word of law and order throughout the four corners of the world.

That's why I was so interested in reading *Golf Club Bible*. It covers every aspect of the game and, in simple terms, allows the reader to follow its evolution, explaining the whys and wherefores of this extraordinary sport. But more than that, it also covers every aspect of the tricky business of finding the right clubs to help your game move forward, something every golfer—whether a novice or one who already loves the game—needs. I have even picked up the odd tip myself!

"Good Golfing!"

Peter Alliss

Introduction

The history of golf clubs goes back hundreds of years, and over time the equipment has changed frequently. This book aims to give the reader a step-by-step guide to the process of selecting the correct golf equipment—from height and hand size, to materials, center-of-gravity positioning and shaft flex.

A player may carry only 14 clubs in his or her bag but has a choice of hundreds, so it's important to get it right in order to save time and money.

Custom fitting is explored in depth; technique has less impact if the equipment used isn't suitable. Every professional in the world has his or her clubs custom fit to their swing, fine-tuning their equipment in a fitting center with computers. This gives them the best opportunity in competition and the comfort of knowing that the equipment is perfect for them.

Like most sports, it boils down to money. The pro golfer wants to score better so that he or she can earn more prize money. Golf club manufacturers want the pros to play well with their equipment for obvious reasons: Their equipment will receive greater exposure in the media, which will increase product sales. They want to produce clubs that are easier for the average golfer to use. With increasing numbers of people taking up the game around the world, there are millions of golfers who are happy to buy the next cutting-edge club if they think it can knock a shot or two off their handicap.

Personal choice
With so many club options available, finding the right mix can be difficult. This selection has an even spread of woods, irons, wedges and a putter.

Ping driver Ping is one of the most innovative golf manufacturers, keeping in step with the rapid changes in equipment. Their drivers have been a popular choice of both pros and amateurs for many years.

This book looks at golf clubs in general, how they work and how the game has changed in recent years. It also includes:

- How clubs have changed in appearance as well as design
- In-depth discussions of each individual club and the purpose of its design
- How the introduction of "new" clubs (e.g., hybrids and 60° wedges) have influenced the game

The main goal is to give clear and concise practical information to help the modern golfer, whether he or she is a novice with a 28 handicap who plays once a month or an avid scratch golfer who wants to play every day. In the end, enjoying the game of golf is what is really essential.

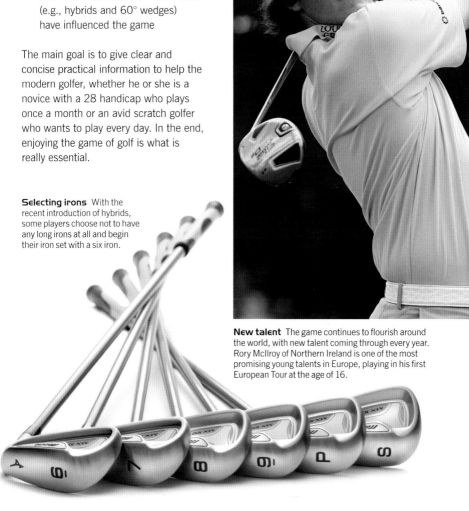

Selecting irons With the recent introduction of hybrids, some players choose not to have any long irons at all and begin their iron set with a six iron.

New talent The game continues to flourish around the world, with new talent coming through every year. Rory McIlroy of Northern Ireland is one of the most promising young talents in Europe, playing in his first European Tour at the age of 16.

The History of Golf Clubs

Golf clubs have been produced for more than 400 years. The earliest were handmade in Scotland, and by modern standards look very strange:

- A long "nose" was used for driving
- Fairway clubs were for medium-range shots
- Spoons were used for shorter shots
- Niblicks were equivalent to today's modern wedges
- A putting cleek was similar to a present-day putter

Clubhead construction consisted mostly of beech, and the shafts were made from ash or hazel. The two pieces were connected via a splint that was bound together tightly using leather straps. These clubs were not available to everyone, only to a lucky few who could afford such an expensive piece of handcrafted equipment.

Pitching niblicks Bunker shots and pitching were more difficult to achieve with these heavy clubs, as spin and feel were much harder to create.

The earliest sign of clubs beginning to change occurred in 1750 when club makers began using metal for niblicks to help improve their durability and avoid frequent breakages. In 1826, manufacturers experimented with hickory for the production of shafts, which was quickly preferred because of its strength. By 1900, persimmon was being imported from the United States to replace beech and other hard woods, and was used to construct clubheads. One alternative was aluminum. In 1902, the first groove-faced irons were introduced, in an attempt to increase spin.

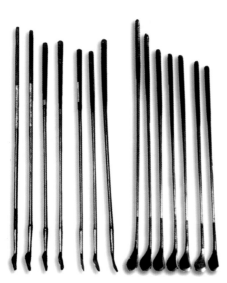

Handmade clubs Before modern machinery took over, many hours were spent on handcrafting golf clubs. This process made each club slightly different.

Although experimentation with steel shafts occurred as early as the 1890s, their use was made legal only in 1929, soon after the first major tournament—the 1931 U.S. Open—was won using steel shafts. Up to the present day, iron heads are either cast or forged steel with steel or graphite shafts. Drivers are usually titanium with graphite shafts. Because of their smaller size, the vast majority of fairway woods have steel heads.

Old Tom Morris Prior to 1900, Tom Morris was the most influential figure in golf. Besides being a fantastic player, he was also a club maker, greenskeeper and golf course designer.

Adjustable loft In some early designs of adjustable golf clubs, the head angle could be altered when facing different shots. Though this has never been popular with golfers, some manufacturers continue to produce these designs.

Ping Eye 2 First manufactured in 1982, the Ping Eye 2 was years ahead of its time due to its cavity-back design and performance. Even today, Ping produces sets of the Ping Eye 2 for sale.

The Modern Game

Though the construction and appearance of modern golf equipment is superficially similar to that of decades ago, there have been many developments that have endeavored to make the game a more modern sport. This chapter highlights different aspects of golf, including drivers, club shafts, courses and scoring, and explains how the changes over the years have brought us the game we know today.

The new face of golf Australian Adam Scott is one of the youngest players in the top 25. Like many golfers these days, his resume is not limited to tournaments, but includes charity foundations and course design.

Changes in the Modern Game

In all sports, there are defining moments that create a new era, when the "modern" game begins. When we talk about modern golf, there are many different aspects to consider. The impact of players is key, but golf clubs, balls and even courses must also be taken into account.

Players tend to define changes in most sports, and this is especially true in golf. In the 1960s, Americans Jack Nicklaus and Arnold Palmer brought golf into the "modern" era. These players added a special something to the game that hadn't been seen before, attacking golf courses with a "no fear" attitude. It was exciting to see young men bring flair to a game that was previously considered a "gentleman's" sport and really only for the wealthy and privileged few.

More changes came in the late 1990s with an African-American player named Eldrick Tont Woods—otherwise known

Gary Player Perhaps more than any other, Player epitomizes the modern golfer. He is the true touring international athlete, traveling a staggering 14 million miles along the way, was a forerunner in endorsements, and is a renowned course architect.

as Tiger. Even after Nicklaus and Palmer had brought the average man into the game, golf was still seen as a "white" sport. In fact, it was only in 1961 that the Professional Golfers' Association (PGA) lifted their notorious "Caucasian clause," which banned any non-Caucasian player from membership. Tiger has undoubtedly changed the way golf is perceived, making it a "cool" sport that everyone—from inner-city kids to movie stars—wants to play. Even his contract for equipment and clothes is with Nike, which is perceived as a trendy and youthful brand.

Tiger Woods Regarded by some as the best golfer ever to have picked up a club, Tiger Woods has more wins than any other active player and is catching up on Jack Nicklaus' total of major wins, with 14.

Maria Kostina Golf has seen a dramatic rise in popularity in eastern Europe in the past decade after a ban during communist rule. In 2007 Kostina became the first Russian, male or female, to play in a major golf championship when she competed in the U.S. Women's Open.

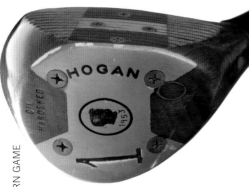

Persimmon woods These clubs gave an amazing feel, but were very difficult to use. In addition, maintaining a varnished, scratch-free persimmon was very time-consuming.

Clubs

Golfers can now hit the ball farther, and this single factor has led to the implementation of many changes in golf clubs over the past 10–15 years. It wasn't long ago when players were teeing it up with a wooden-headed driver—either a persimmon or a laminate.

Persimmon

A persimmon was hand-carved from a block of wood. It was a prized possession, its great expense due to the hours and craftsmanship put in to create such a club. However, because of the nature of wood, the clubs were difficult to keep in pristine condition and became damaged extremely easily, particularly if the wood wasn't dried properly after playing in the rain.

In addition, wood is actually quite light when it is the size of a driver, so the only way to increase the weight was first to remove the base plate (on the sole) and then drill specific-size holes in the wood and fill them with molten lead. The lead would dry and remain in the

wood and thus increase the weight. Finally, the wood would always be varnished in order to try to protect it and to give the club a classy finish, but any golfer playing regularly had to revarnish the persimmon at least once a year.

Laminate

The alternative and cheaper option was to buy a "laminate" wood. These clubs were also made of wood, but compressed chips were used instead of a solid block. This obviously made the cost of this club far lower, as they were mass produced by machines as opposed to the handmade persimmons. Laminate woods were spray-painted, usually black, and then varnished on top. The feel was slightly harder, but the look was completely different.

Steel Ten to 15 years ago, nearly all clubs were made from steel. With the introduction of other materials in clubmaking, it is now rare to have so many steel clubheads in one bag.

BIG BERTHA

Soon after the steel explosion, manufacturers looked for a new material for the next "wonder club" that would make every player hit the ball much farther and straighter. Making steel-headed clubs bigger was problematic, as the clubs became much too heavy and impossible to swing.

Callaway overcame this with the production of a steel-headed driver called "Big Bertha." The walls of the club were thinned out so that its overall weight was

First oversize driver
The original Big Bertha by Callaway was the first oversize driver to hit the market. The club's sales soared as golfers benefited from its playability.

Modern drivers The modern Big Bertha is more than twice the size in cubic centimeters than the original. It is made from titanium and offers a much higher degree of consistency.

actually the same, but the size of the head was increased considerably. At first, a club of this size was an eyesore—it looked too big. In terms of performance, however, it was much better than anything else on the market and became a huge success. Players soon got used to the size of the head, and then anything else just looked too small. The main problem with a thin-walled steel driver was that the club could be dented or misshapen easily.

A persimmon block oozed class—all the top pros used them—whereas a laminate was cheaper but also looked it.

Steel

Steel-headed woods were introduced in the mid-1980s. By using steel, the manufacturers could produce clubs that had larger sweet spots, thus making it easier to hit a good shot. Players could

attack the ball with more confidence. Because steel is relatively heavy, the size of the heads didn't increase much either, and a steel-headed wood had virtually no upkeep; it had a sandblasted finish that made the surface resistant to scratches and dents, and it didn't need to be revarnished. These metal-headed clubs could be mass produced at a reasonable cost to the public.

Titanium

The "space age" metal titanium allowed golf manufacturers to build their large-headed, thin-walled drivers with ease. Titanium is extremely strong and light, so much so that drivers became larger and larger. Because golfers were now used to big heads, previous problems of clubs looking too big were long forgotten. And due to the bigger sweet spots in the clubheads, even below-average golfers could have a greater degree of success with a poor shot. Each new model that a manufacturer produced seemed bigger than the previous one, until only a few years ago when golf's two regulatory

Titanium driver With the introduction of titanium, clubheads could be increased in size without increasing the weight because of titanium's combination of lightness and strength.

bodies—the United States Golf Association (USGA) and the Royal and Ancient Golf

WHAT SHAPE PRODUCES OPTIMUM BALL FLIGHT?

With the use of modern equipment, such as launch monitors and swing-analysis machines, it has been concluded that the optimum ball flight that produces the most distance is a rainbow shape, high in launch and low in spin. The theory behind this is that the longer a player can keep the ball in the air without it stalling, the farther the ball travels. The high launch gives immediate height and

the low amount of spin stops the ball from stalling. There are obvious factors to take into account. Swing speed is paramount, as this changes the launch angle and the amount of spin needed. Before the modern era of golf, the preferred ball flight for better players was a ball that started quite low and then rose as the spin kicked in, creating a pretty-looking shot that landed very softly but lacked power.

Optimum ball flight The rainbow shape is the optimum ball flight for golfers using a driver. A high launch with little spin keeps the ball in the air, creating more carry and distance.

Club of St. Andrews (R&A) in Scotland—limited the cubic capacity of a driver.

Thin faces: It wasn't only the size of the sweet spots that made titanium clubs so popular; there was a period of time when manufacturers were making drivers with extremely thin faces, creating a trampoline effect on the face so that the ball was almost bouncing off the club. This increased distance when struck correctly, however, golfers found the average distance from a shot varied so much that they weren't getting the

consistency they required. Furthermore, the USGA and R&A placed a limit on how much spring a face could have. With this restriction in place, there was now very little left for companies to do to increase distance—effectively, clubs had reached their limit. The manufacturers had to take a different approach, focusing more on accuracy through spin and launch angle.

Distance is key: With modern launch monitors, manufacturers have established how to produce straighter shots using spin and how to change the weight around in order to make the ball fly differently. By achieving a certain spin and launch angle, players can maximize distance.

Composites
Manufacturers have now begun to make driver heads composite. In most cases, the face and front half of the driver head is constructed from titanium, as it receives the most stress. The rear part of the head is made from graphite, which is very light, and because the heads are hollow, the manufacturers can easily add weight to the rear of the head and the bottom of the club. This moves the center of gravity lower and farther back, which produces the best flight.

Classic look Drivers have increased in size dramatically in the past 15 years, but the pear shape remains the same.

Composite drivers Manufacturers have started to introduce titanium-composite drivers where the face is titanium for strength and the rest of the head is graphite to allow more variation in weight distribution.

Balls

The golf ball has also changed considerably over the past 10 to 15 years. The low-rising, high-spinning ball flight mentioned above was needed because the highest-spinning balls, which were covered in balata (nonelastic rubber), had very short life spans. Top pros changed their ball every two or three holes, some as often as every hole. But players continued to use these balata balls, because when chipping, pitching and putting, they gave off a soft feel, also helping golfers judge distance.

For players who required more distance, there was always the option of a harder ball. The ball would have a harder cover and different dimple pattern, and this would reduce backspin and increase distance. But the downside of the harder cover was that the "feel" aspect of the game—involving anything that doesn't require a full swing—was very difficult to execute because the pebblelike ball coating would cause the ball almost to spring off the clubface. This was a good option if you were a higher-handicap golfer and distance is what you strove for, but lower-handicap players generally needed the extra feel from a ball to help them score well in their short games.

The PRO V1

Golf manufacturers attempted to create a ball that appealed to both types of handicaps. In 2000, Titleist produced a ball called the PRO V1. It had an unbelievable launch into the market; weeks before

EVOLUTION OF THE GOLF BALL

The earliest golf ball was covered in leather, stuffed with goose or chicken feathers and called a "feathery." These balls were relatively expensive, but continued to be used for almost 400 years. However, with the development of space-age plastics, silicone and improved rubber, modern balls create more distance, spin, control and consistency.

Titleist PRO V1 This ball's three-piece multilayer construction maximizes distance without losing control, and provides excellent durability.

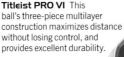

the ball's launch tour, professionals were winning with it, and it received enthusiastic coverage in the press and on TV. It was targeted at the single figure and scratch handicapper, but such was the hype that everyone was suddenly using this ball.

The PRO V1 did everything a good golfer required from a ball. It was proven to go longer than the high-spinning balata, but with almost the exact same spin rate on shorter shots. Though the PRO V1 came at a premium, costing around 25 percent more than other balls, its cover was much more durable. Ultimately, this single golf ball wiped out the balata ball, and today nearly all golf ball manufacturers have their own version.

Shafts

Around 100 years ago, golf shafts were made from wood, which was the only practical material available at that time. Twenty years ago, most shafts were made from steel. Today, probably 100 percent of pros use steel-shafted irons (which are used to score, not for distance). Steel is easy to manipulate and has very little torque, or twist, so when putting shafts in a set of irons, it's important to have all the shafts reacting the same way. This consistency outweighs the slight extra weight that comes with steel. Steel is also relatively inexpensive.

Graphite

The biggest leap in shaft production has been the use of graphite. When first introduced 20 years ago, graphite windings were of a poor, inconsistent quality and manufacturers found it difficult to mass-produce them. In addition, graphite shafts had a large amount of torque, causing the shafts to twist. This became a golf club manufacturer's worst nightmare. The last thing a player wants is any twist in the club; stability

Shaft options Steel and graphite are the most popular and effective materials for shaft construction.

is key. The idea to use graphite in shafts was correct, however. More swing, power and distance can ultimately be achieved because graphite is a lighter material and more weight can be placed in the head to balance the club.

Today, the process of graphite shaft production has improved, and companies now produce graphite shafts with very little torque. These shafts perform almost as well as steel during tests, and now, 99 percent of all drivers sold have a graphite shaft. This is completely distance related: A graphite shaft is as stable as steel but weighs considerably less, allowing players to swing with greater power.

Titanium

The third shaft option is titanium. Though titanium is light, stable and has low torque, is it very expensive. Companies have attempted to manufacture clubs with titanium shafts, but the cost of the club nearly doubled and as a result its use never really took off.

Swing

If players have the confidence to hit the ball harder, they will do so. Over a period of a generation, the physical size of the touring pro has changed: players are taller, physically stronger and more flexible. This allows a swing to turn more, thus generating more power. A swing's accuracy and control are no longer as important as they were 20 years ago; power is what matters most. All modern golf swings have big shoulder turns and less hand action, and all modern pros need to be able to hit the ball 300 yards through the air.

In the past 10 to 15 years, players such as Nick Faldo, Fred Couples, Seve Ballesteros and Ian Woosnam all had very different swings and body shapes compared to the players of today—Tiger Woods, Adam Scott, Retief Goosen and Padraig Harrington, to name just a few. These active players have a greater understanding and level of physical fitness and produce very powerful golf swings.

Seve Ballesteros Though not known for his power or accuracy, Seve's flair, imagination and touch around the greens have earned him five major victories and many other wins on the tour.

Retief Goosen Blessed with an elegant, slow swing that oozes style, Retief Goosen doesn't seem powerful initially, but he delivers great clubhead speed, producing long drives.

Courses

More powerful swings and increased distance have led to changes in the structure of golf courses. Once pros began hitting the ball farther, the scoring inevitably got better, so much so that courses built 20 years ago suddenly had no defenses against the stronger players. If we look at PGA tournaments from the mid- to late-1990s, for example, scoring records were being broken almost every week.

Playing doglegs, where previously players hit to the corner and then hit their approach shot from there, were now a different game; the pros would simply hit over the dogleg, reducing the hole by

Augusta National Home of the Masters, the Augusta National Golf Club in Georgia has evolved to keep up with the game. The length of the course remained almost constant for 50 years, but has gradually gained over 500 yards (457 m) since 2001.

vast amounts of yardage. Bunkers, lakes, trees and any other types of hazards that were previously placed to catch a loose or slightly mishit tee shot were now obsolete. Estimates suggest that the major courses around the world have each been extended up to 15 percent in length and have added around 20 new bunkers or hazards. There have even been changes at local golf clubs, from creating extra bunkers or extended tees to planting more thickets of trees.

Valderrama at San Roque Regularly voted the best course in continental Europe, Valderrama is a challenging course for pros and amateurs alike. The course has had a number of changes to the design over the past decade, with bunkers made even bigger, trees moved to intrude on the line to the green.

The Westin Hotel Golf Course at Macau New golf courses in expanding markets, such as this magnificent course at a resort in Macau, China, cater to the long-driving abilities of modern golfers.

Outlook on Custom Fitting

Going back 10 or 15 years, an amateur golfer who needed a new set of clubs went to a store to have a look around, possibly tried one or two out and then made a decision to purchase a set. Only recently have nonprofessional golfers even considered the idea of custom fitting, when in fact it is more beneficial to the average golfer than it is to a seasoned pro.

The less golfing ability someone has, the more important custom fitting is. A professional has the feel and expertise to alter his or her swing to suit different clubs, so even if the equipment isn't perfect for them, the pro can still produce excellent shots. But if an amateur golfer bought clubs that were too short, for example, he or she would find it extremely difficult to overcome the difference in length.

In the past, it was difficult for golfers to find places that offered a custom fitting service. The cost involved could also be prohibitive. If a player sought the advice of a pro to find out if their clubs needed to be adjusted, the pro would charge a fitting fee on top of any other charges, such as club lengthening or lie adjustment.

Swing analysis Colin Montgomerie has his swing analyzed at the Callaway facility in California. Swing analysis is part of the club fitting procedure and is suitable for professionals and recreational golfers alike.

Ping

In the mid- to late-1990s, only one main golf manufacturer offered a full custom-fitting option when purchasing a set of clubs: Ping. However, a golfer first had to decide that Ping clubs were their definite choice and they then had to arrange a fitting session at the factory, which could involve a waiting time of two months. Once the golfer had confirmed the appointment and made the trip to the factory, Ping would construct the custom fit set for the golfer to take away—an excellent result, but a long process.

Ping putter Introduced in 1966, the Ping putter is the most popular and successful putter in the world, with more than 2,000 tournament wins to its name.

Shot analysis With the use of computers and launch monitors, every shot can be analyzed in detail, so that clubs are perfectly fitted to each individual player.

Today

Gradually, more manufacturers realized that custom fitting was essential for their customers. Initially, these golf club manufacturers created custom-fitting packages, which retail outlets stocked in their stores. A package usually contained every model of iron that the manufacturer produced. There were up to five or six different specifications for each iron, consisting of a range of different shaft flexes in both steel and graphite, and choices in lie one or two in both flat and upright options. A selection of grip options were also contained in the package, dependent on hand size.

These packages allowed PGA professionals to do the custom fitting on site, resulting in

the same outcome as if the customer had gone to the factory. This was a much quicker and simpler solution for the customer, who could have a set of new custom-fit clubs in their bag within two weeks. This service is available at most golf retail outlets today, though the major golf companies also have custom fitting services in their factories as an added option.

Ping irons One of the leading brands in golf for many years, Ping has built a reputation on producing top quality products with an excellent feel and look.

The Equipment Explained

Although golf equipment has changed over the years, the principle has remained the same—the desire to hit the ball to create height and distance while also having control over its direction. Custom fitting is important, but the final decision when purchasing equipment comes down to personal preference, taking all factors into account. Heavy clubs and soft grips might work for one golfer but not for another.

Tools of the trade Three million golfers leave the game every year in North America because they are frustrated with their game: The more we know about the basic tools of golf, the better we can use them to our advantage.

An Introduction to Golf Clubs

For the novice golfer, starting out can be a scary prospect. Like most sports, it looks very easy when the professionals play, but it is important to realize that even at the early stages, the selection of clubs is key.

Before you hit a golf ball, take a lesson or play on a course, it makes sense to get familiar with your clubs. Simply holding a club gives a beginner an idea of what the club is like, from appearance to weight and balance. Initially, holding it might feel strange, as the weight is toward the end—in the head—and it is common that beginners without any prior racket-sports experience injure their wrists. Although there are many different aspects to swinging a golf club, the only part of the body in direct contact with it is the hands, so this automatically causes the wrists to take the strain.

In previous generations, due to the high cost of clubs, most golfers had equipment passed down through the family. In modern times, with better quality components and budget equipment now available, it is better to buy new or secondhand.

Information about golf clubs is available everywhere; the Internet, retail outlets and PGA professionals are all a valuable source of sound advice.

Club options Though there are many options when composing a set, one driver, one fairway wood, one hybrid, seven irons, three wedges and one putter are the most popular choices.

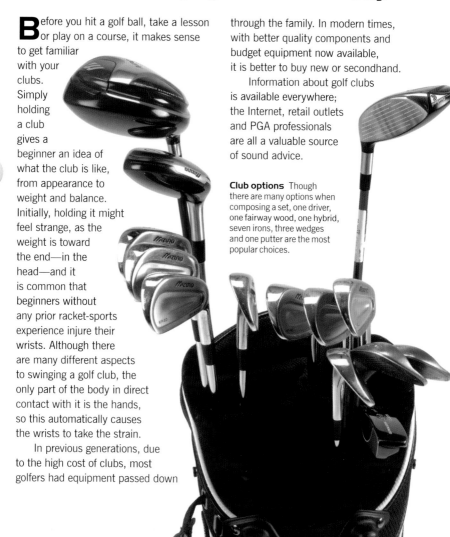

THE PARTS OF THE CLUB

Shaft: Usually steel or graphite; extends from the head up to the grip

Ferrule: Small plastic object that fits snugly to the top of the hosel around the shaft; has no function and is only for cosmetic purposes

Hosel: Small section of steel coming from the heel area where the shaft is secured

Heel: The side of the clubface closest to the hosel

Toe: The side of the clubface farthest from the hosel

Sole: The part of the club that rests on the ground at address

Top edge: The top of the clubface as seen from above or from the address position

Leading edge: The bottom of the clubface and usually the part of the clubhead that is farthest forward at address

Face: The area between the heel, toe, leading edge and top edge—the hitting area of the club

Body: The area behind the face; usually hollow in drivers

Sweet spot: The exact center of the face, where the ball reacts best

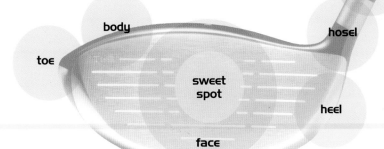

driver

wood

hybrid

How do Clubs Work?

Distance in golf is related to clubhead speed, so the faster the club is moving as it strikes the ball, the faster the ball comes off the face. This combined with the loft and amount of spin generated on the ball will determine how far the ball travels.

Ball speed is the initial speed when the ball comes off the face. It is measured at 1.4 times clubhead speed; for example, a clubhead speed of 100 mph (160 kph) produces a ball speed of 140 mph (225 kph).

Although golf is known as a "feel" sport, strength is also a factor, especially when focusing on creating ball speed. Hitting the ball harder increases its speed, but strength alone is not the ultimate answer. Having a lighter shaft or a lighter clubhead gives the player the advantage of swinging a

lighter object. By swinging with the same force, a golfer can increase clubhead speed without actually increasing effort.

Swinging the club with more control and less aggression also helps to return the clubface square to the target and produce a shot toward the intended direction. It is important to find this zone—swinging too slowly increases accuracy but reduces distance, and swinging too hard increases distance but with a consequent loss of direction. The key to golf is found somewhere in the middle.

iron

wedge

putter

A club for every purpose The appearance of golf clubs differs from model to model because of the specific requirements for which they were devised, but the general purpose for all clubs remain the same—to create a specific flight and distance.

Launch Angle

The ball speed alone creates distance, but a player can utilize this even more by creating a perfect launch angle.

Through the use of launch monitor technology, an optimum launch has been found for every ball speed. If a player achieves this launch angle, they get the perfect ball flight. The basic concept is this: The more ball speed created, the lower launch a player requires. A scratch golfer producing a ball speed of around 140 mph (225 kph) requires a launch angle of approximately 14°. Any greater and the ball rockets into the sky without

WHAT IS LAUNCH ANGLE?

The launch angle is the angle at which the ball leaves the clubface when hit off the ground. Momentum, spin and stance are just a few factors that can affect the launch angle.

enough forward momentum and loses potential distance. Conversely, if the launch angle is too small, the ball will not stay in the air long enough and will lose distance as a result. The same principle applies with a more novice golfer. A player with a ball speed of 90 mph (145 kph) requires a much higher launch angle, somewhere closer to 20°.

The launch angle changes with the amount of power in the shot. With a lower ball speed the ball does not stay in the air as long, so a higher launch angle helps keep the ball up for longer, producing more distance from the shot. This is why different players require different lofts to help produce optimum launch and flight. As every golfer has his or her own individual swing, this process always requires time and patience until the correct loft is found.

Launch The ball comes off Nick Faldo's club at a small angle with very little launch and divot. This indicates that a long iron is being used.

WHAT IS LOFT?

Loft is a measurement of the angle of the clubface. It determines how high and fast a ball can travel. Drivers have low loft, while wedges have a greater loft.

Spin

Golf clubs produce spin, and spin is what helps a ball rise and stay in the air. Spin can be affected in two different ways. The first is clubhead speed: The faster a club is moving at impact, the more ball speed is created. As spin is produced on every shot, more ball speed creates more spin. This is why better players tend to produce more spin—they strike the ball with more force. Most amateurs would love to create backspin, but unless they strike the ball with precision and power, this is unlikely.

The second way to produce more spin is in the angle of attack. By striking down on the ball more, the ball stays on the clubface at impact slightly longer and rolls up the face that little bit more, creating more spin. This can be proved in different swings. If a player tends to swing the club with a steeper action, it is likely to create a steeper attack on to the ball, thus imparting a lot of spin. However, a player with a much flatter plane tends to strike the ball cleanly without a divot—this results in less spin.

There are benefits for both types of swing. A player who spins the ball more is able to hit the ball higher and stop it more quickly on the green, and so prefers harder greens and less wind. But a player who creates less spin prefers a course with more wind and softer greens, as the lower amount of spin creates a lower ball flight.

Backspin Hitting down into the ball with a successful combination of loft and strike produces the correct trajectory with backspin, helping maintain control.

Topspin Striking the ball above the equator causes very little or no lift, as loft does not take effect. In some extreme cases the clubface's lack of contact with the ball results in almost no backspin and instead creates topspin.

Low launch Tiger Woods uses a long iron to keep the ball initially quite low to the ground. The club simply brushes into the ground and does not cause a divot.

FLEX

The club's shaft flexes in two places during the swing. A slight lag in the clubhead is created when the player starts the downswing. Just before impact, when the wrists start to uncock, the clubhead catches up and actually overtakes the hands. This is known as the shaft "kicking" and is the second time that the shaft bends during the swing.

The amount of bend depends on the strength of the player and the speed of the swing.

Stiffness Though a driver and iron shaft may be categorized with the same flex rating, the actual amount of bend in the shaft will increase as the length of shaft increases.

Wind

The wind has a significant effect on shots, and is very difficult to judge when playing. A lower ball flight into the wind affects the ball much less than a higher-flighted shot. Alternatively, when hitting downwind, a low ball flight is affected less by the wind than by the higher-flighted shot.

However, there are instances when hitting downwind, that the ball can almost get knocked down in a particularly strong wind. Spinning the ball in the wind makes a misdirected shot even worse. This is why better golfers choose a shorter backswing and follow through into the wind, as this keeps the ball down. Known as a "punch shot," it should be used only in the wind, or if the golfer is in trouble and a low shot is required. Combining this firm-wristed follow-through with a ball position located much farther back in the player's stance, the result is a low-flighted shot with less spin. This tactic can be seen a lot more in Europe, where the courses are windier generally and with firmer fairways, and where sometimes a low running shot is preferred to a high, soft landing shot.

Wind drag
Because driver heads have become bigger and bigger over the past decade—to the extent that the PGA and R&A now have strict rules about size—manufacturers have realized that players start to feel some resistance when swinging the club, which is called wind drag. Though the ball is on the clubface for only a split second, the ball reacts to the positioning of the face, so any small degree of misalignment can result in wayward shots.

Stability
This relates to how stable the clubhead is at impact. If the club has any type of twisting at impact, the clubface either opens or closes and produces a slice or a hook. Because clubheads are made of steel or titanium, it is unlikely that any twisting is caused by them. The weakness is in the shaft.

All shafts twist at impact, but it's how much they twist that spells the difference between good and great shafts. Steel shafts are very stable and produce very little twist, and this is the main reason that professionals tend to choose steel over graphite in their irons.

Graphite is slightly harder to get right. Because of its composition, there is always an element of torque. When graphite shafts were first introduced, the

torque was so high that any consistency was impossible. But as manufacturers improved the quality of graphite shafts, they have become more stable and twist far less, thus becoming more "playable."

Using the Right Ball
When struck correctly, golf clubs produce a fantastic ball flight, but this also has something to do with the type of ball used.

Modern golf balls go through hundreds of tests to make sure they are the correct shape, compression and size, and that the dimple pattern is consistent. However, years ago, when balls were smaller, softer and stuffed full of feathers, golfers couldn't rely on consistency—a perfectly struck shot could easily travel half its distance owing to the quality of the ball.

As time passed, designers figured out that a ball's dimple pattern had a huge effect on its flight. By experimenting with different patterns, it was concluded that spin could also be affected. This helped with the marketing of golf balls; better players choose higher-spinning balls, while more novice golfers prefer the low-spin options.

The smallest imperfection on a ball can easily affect a shot, from a piece of mud to a miniscule scratch. This is why professionals use new balls frequently and get them cleaned at every opportunity.

Dimple patterns Dimples are required for distance and stability. There are between 300–500 dimples on one ball. Manufacturers produce a range of balls with different dimple designs to suit their construction; this differs from manufacturer to manufacturer.

The Driver

The driver, although used on average no more than 14 times in a round, is one of the most important clubs you will purchase. It's the longest club in the bag, which makes it the hardest to control, and its extra length creates a bigger arc in the swing. Consequently, the ball travels a greater distance than with any other club. A good driver sets the tone for a round, so it makes sense to choose it wisely.

The driver, or number 1 wood, is one of the most reviewed clubs in the bag, and golf club manufacturers have been competing for years to create the perfect prototype in terms of maximum distance and accuracy. The general appearance of the driver hasn't changed much over the years, but the move toward steel, then titanium, then composite heads, has led to investments in the millions in the manufacturers' strive for perfection. This, combined with the introduction of several different types of shafts, has led to an overwhelming and sometimes confusing choice for the would-be buyer. As with all clubs, knowing how the driver is made gives you a greater understanding of how it works and helps you find the right one to suit your game.

Heads

Wooden-headed drivers were known to be difficult to hit and very high maintenance, with regular refurbishments needed to maintain its appearance—the state of the face, sole and head would take a beating after a season's play.

The change to steel improved durability, but the heads were still small and heavy, so manufacturers made the

Internal weighting Huge heads are made hollow in order to reduce weight, but this also allows manufacturers to place the weight in the optimum position without it being visible.

steel thinner, which allowed the heads to be bigger without being heavier. The larger head size made driving the ball easier. The floodgates were then opened as companies clamored to find new materials to make the biggest, most powerful drivers they could, and along came titanium.

Titanium-headed drivers were lighter than steel and even stronger. So the heads could be bigger—at an increase of up to one third in size—with the extra-thin walls making the heads even easier to hit. However, having the ease of a titanium-headed driver does come at a high cost.

KEY FEATURES

TOE

Some drivers are weighted less at the toe end than at the heel. This encourages the toe to move more quickly than the heel, resulting in fewer sliced shots.

FACE

Many modern drivers have the grooves removed from the sweet spot. The smooth finish on the face helps with the reduction of spin and can improve distance.

SOLE

A driver's sole is usually rounded to help reduce wind drag during the swing. In addition, if the ground is struck, the design forces the club to almost bounce off the ground rather than dig in.

ADDRESS

Most drivers have a marking on top of the head showing the center of the face, making it easier to set up the ball. This also ensures that the clubface is aiming at the target.

The shape of the driver has stayed much the same since the birth of golf—it has always been the biggest club in size, volume and depth, thus proving that the original design was the best one. Square-shaped heads have been introduced recently with the concept that by having corners, the weight can be distributed farther behind the heel and toe of the club, giving less twist and producing a more consistent ball flight. Though the science is correct, many believe that the shape of the head has proven to be too dramatic, and most golfers still prefer the original pear shape.

TaylorMade Tour Burner
This driver has a 450cc head with a deep face for a higher launch. It's light shaft leads to greater clubhead speed.

Ping GIO This driver has a 460cc head with a slightly thinner crown allowing the weight to be distrbuted elsewhere. The center of gravity is improved, which gives a higher launch and reduced spin.

TaylorMade r7 SuperQuad This 460cc driver has an unusual black head with four movable weights, allowing the player to change trajectory and launch angle. It's low, deep center of gravity promotes long hitting.

Mizuno MX700
This driver has a slightly longer look at the back of the club but is still 460cc. Many modern drivers are very loud because of their hollow heads, but this model includes a vibration-dampening hull that makes it seem more solid and less noisy.

Callaway Big Bertha Diablo This driver is 460cc and 100 percent titanium. With no hosel, the weight is repositioned in the perimeter of the clubhead to add stability.

Callaway FT IQ This driver is 460cc in size, with a face that is angled one degree closed. The carbon body, titanium face and square shape allow the weight distribution to perfect the center of gravity for maximum distance.

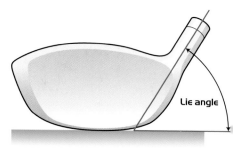

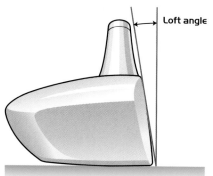

Driver angles The lie of a driver is between 57° and 61° depending on the manufacturer and the design of the club. Lofts tend to be more consistent, ranging from 7° to 12°.

Titanium is found in beach sand throughout the world, especially in Australia and China, but mining it is not an easy process, and this in turn causes it to be more expensive than steel. In addition, titanium must be cast in a vacuum. This is expensive because many clubheads don't come out in perfect condition and must be destroyed.

Most titanium woods are made using very lightweight graphite shafts. The lighter and more stable the shaft, the more difficult they are to produce and the more expensive they become.

Loft

Loft is an important and often overlooked factor to bear in mind with this club. The ranges of lofts available in drivers have remained constant—anywhere from 7° up to 12°—though modern titanium drivers actually hit the ball much higher than either steel- or wooden-headed drivers. The amount of loft you need depends on the spin you produce. The faster your club moves at impact, the greater the spin, so you need less loft to stop the ball from ballooning up, resulting in a shorter distance. If your spin is slower, you need more loft to add spin to your shot in order to compensate for the lack of spin provided by the clubhead speed. This keeps the ball in the air and helps with distance. Variations in loft occur, which is why every player should be custom-fit for each club.

Distance is enhanced when creating a high launch with low spin, so it is now common to find most titanium drivers have few or no groove marks on the center of the clubface, because this will help reduce the amount of spin.

Teeing up It is important to tee the ball high when using modern drivers. The player should strike the ball on the up to help reduce spin and then launch it from the top third area of the face.

This reflects the average loft of a player's driver—a typical golfer with a steel- or wooden-headed driver needs 11 or 12° of loft. With titanium heads, that loft is closer to 10°.

The way a ball is teed up has also changed. Before the introduction of titanium, the ball was teed relatively low to encourage a downward strike into the back. This created a very low launch and a lot of spin, which we now know isn't the best ball flight for long distances. Today, with the combination of bigger heads with deeper faces and the requirement of a higher launch and less spin, balls are teed very high to help encourage the player to almost hit up on the ball, thus reducing spin but increasing launch angle.

Shaft weight Though Sergio Garcia is not powerfully built, he has a very fast and powerful swing, creating incredible clubhead speed with a big shoulder turn on the backswing.

Shafts

Shafts can vary, and you will struggle if you use the wrong type. The three main factors to keep in mind are:

- Weight
- Flex
- Torque

Weight

Less flexible, heavier steel shafts give you more accuracy than graphite, but lighter graphite shafts can give you greater distance. Titanium shafts today are up to two or three inches longer than the steel versions 10 years ago. This added length also helps with distance, as the club can be swung on a bigger arc, creating more power, since it is farther from the ball. These days it's rare for any player to have steel shafts in their driver.

Golfers want to create distance, and players tend to swing much harder with a driver than with any other club in their bag.

The look of a driver is thought to increase confidence: The bigger head makes the ball look smaller and appear easier to hit. The club is also built for distance. This is why it is acceptable to have a slightly stiffer shaft in a driver than in the rest of the set. Most drivers, steel or titanium, have a hosel to support the shaft where it enters the head. This is believed to help stabilize the shaft; the shaft usually goes down around two thirds into the clubhead and, thanks to modern adhesives, stays there. Some manufacturers have produced designs where the shaft actually goes all the way through the head and is cut flush to the sole of the club. This is also done to create more stability in both the head and the shaft. Visually, many manufactures prefer this, as the requirement for the hosel is no longer needed.

Driver setup When addressing the ball with a driver, the player stands taller because of the length of the club, making him or her automatically swing flatter. Having the ball farther forward in the stance promotes an upward strike, helping with launch and spin.

GRIP

Do not overlook the importance of the grip on a driver. Grips can be adjusted to your particular hand size—players with smaller hand sizes prefer a thinner grip for better feel of the club.

Flex

This is the amount the shaft bends when placed under a load, and it needs to be perfectly suited to your swing speed so that you can deliver the clubface square to the ball. The clubface closes through impact, so it's a very precise action. If the shaft is too flexible, it causes the club to close too soon at impact, resulting in a hooked shot. If it is too stiff, the opposite takes place and the clubface won't have time to close, resulting in an open clubface and a slice. Shaft flex is based on swing speed, so if you're a longer, stronger ball hitter, your swing is faster and a stiffer shaft would normally be required to help stabilize your club. If you have a very slow swing, you'll need a more flexible shaft to help with the closing action of the clubface.

Torque

Torque is the amount of twist in graphite shafts. Unlike steel, which is a more solid material, graphite is made up of strips that can be wound together to give more twist. The correct torque is based on swing speed, feel and ball flight. It depends on the individual, however. Stronger and faster hitters need less torque to stabilize the clubhead, whereas slower hitters need some twist to help them with closing the clubface.

DRIVER STANCE

Swinging the club harder, having more length in the shaft and producing more power is great for distance, but you almost certainly lose control. The solution is to find the driver length you are most comfortable with. The driver produces the most powerful swing from a player, so balance and stability become even more important. This is why a wider stance is adopted.

Shoulders As the body rotates, the right shoulder is lower than the left shoulder. This is because the right hand is farther down the club than the left hand.

Arms A player's arms should be extended out in front, giving enough room to allow all the body weight to shift.

Hips At impact, the hips should have started rotating, allowing the rest of the body to follow and so shift the weight forward.

Hands The right hand should roll over the left hand as the club closes. This action can also create extra clubhead speed at the essential point of impact.

Knees As the hips turn, the right knee turns in, too. This is because the right side of the body transfers its weight across to the left side.

Feet A player's weight shifts onto the left foot, which is slightly splayed out in order to maintain balance.

Clubhead The clubhead should be raised from the ground to ensure a clean strike and also should be positioned square to the target for accuracy.

Fairway Woods

Fairway woods are now considered to be three, five and seven woods, with some manufacturers even going up to a nine wood. As with drivers, there are various lofts available in these different clubs.

A standard three wood has a loft of 15°, but some manufacturers produce a 13° or 14° versions, and others a 16° model. This is based on the market the club is aimed at and the weight of the club. For example, if a three wood is aimed at the novice golfer, its purpose is to create height, so the loft is more likely to be 15° or 16°. Alternatively, a club aimed at the lower-handicap market is more likely to produce a 13° or 14° club, due to the excess clubhead speed, resulting in more spin and a higher flight—this decrease by 1° or 2° less keeps the ball from ballooning.

The options on lofts aren't quite as extensive for five and seven woods as it's generally the more novice golfer who requires these clubs. As long irons and hybrids are also an option, there are far less of these sold than three woods.

Five, seven and even nine woods are used less commonly because golfers now have other options when hitting the

Internal weight Though mostly constructed of steel, fairway woods' heads are hollow and are much smaller than drivers' heads. This allows manufacturers to place weight in specific areas to enhance the playability of the clubs.

ball the distances these clubs provide. However, the design of these fairway woods inspires confidence—a wood shape with a lot of loft looks very easy to hit.

Set of fairway woods Some players prefer to use fairway woods rather than irons or hybrids, due to their forgiving nature. Manufacturers produce fairway woods with lofts of up to 25°.

TOE

Fairway woods are generally longer from heel to toe to help with consistency.

FACE

With a much shallower face than a driver, a fairway wood is easier to strike off the grass than from a tee.

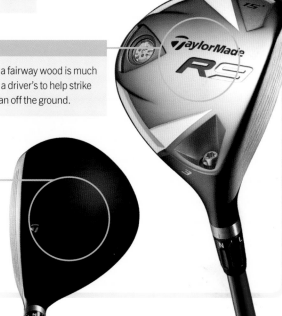

SOLE

The sole of a fairway wood is much flatter than a driver's to help strike the ball clean off the ground.

ADDRESS

At address, it is important to keep the club flat to the ground to encourage consistent strikes and ball flight.

DESIGN

Because fairway woods are required to hit the ball from the ground as well as occasionally from a tee, they have a different design than drivers. The head is much smaller than a driver's and is usually constructed from steel. Initially, when titanium first hit the wood scene, some manufacturers introduced titanium fairway woods, but the heads were almost too big, and though the clubs were excellent off a tee peg, it was extremely difficult to strike a shot from the grass.

There are slight differences in fairway-wood design. Some manufacturers adopt a very shallow face, whereas others have more depth. The shallow-faced fairway woods tend to be quite wide in the face, giving a wider sweet spot, whereas the deeper face has a larger sweet spot depth-wise.

TaylorMade Burner This club has a shallow face and is wide from heel to toe, making it more playable and easier to strike off the ground.

Mizuno F-60 Consisting of an ultrathin titanium crown and a high-tech precision stainless-steel face and body, a low, deep center of gravity is created, ideal for trajectory and ease of launch.

Mizuno MX-700 An extremely strong, thin and lightweight face increases energy transfer and ball speed.

Callaway Diablo
The use of 100 percent stainless steel and a short hosel allows the weight to be placed elsewhere in the head, enabling Callaway to produce draw- and fade-biased heads.

TaylorMade r7 CGB
Interchangeable weights behind the toe and heel enable a player to alter the ball flight.

Ping Rapture V2
This club utilizes a tungsten insert to place the center of gravity farther back and lower, creating a high launch.

Shafts Most fairway woods come with a graphite shaft as standard because the ability to provide distance is a big selling point. Manufacturers test other shafts with their products to find the best two or three head/shaft combinations. These become options when purchasing woods.

Loft

The principles are the same with the more lofted fairway woods: The intended strike is to hit the ball cleanly from the ground and not down into the ball, as the club provides plenty of loft for height. Because the club is designed for distance, a high amount of spin isn't necessary.

Like every other club, fairway woods get shorter in length the more loft they have. When a club has more loft it gives more control. The difference in length between fairway woods is usually one inch (2.5 cm); however, this does vary from manufacturer to manufacturer.

As its name suggests, a fairway club is to be used from the fairway, but golfers can benefit from its design when hitting from the rough; the more lofted fairway woods can generate good distance from poor lies.

Shafts

Fairway wood shafts usually come in graphite to enhance distance and reduce weight. However, some golfers prefer steel to gain a bit more control at a reduced cost. Ladies' and seniors' fairway woods often come with graphite as standard, as the lighter shaft helps generate more clubhead speed.

Loft Fairway woods have varying lofts, and though this may differ by only 1° or 2°, it has a dramatic effect. The three woods shown here vary between 14° and 16° of loft, a subtle change that is visibly noticeable.

14°   15°   16°

Odd vs. Even

Before modern steel-headed fairway clubs were introduced, the fairway wood was very popular and more varieties were available. It was common for players to have the full range of woods, which consisted of two, three, four, five, six and seven, with the common half an inch difference in length between each club. Once the 14-club rule was introduced, this allowed very little room for any other clubs, so golfers tended to have either evens (two, four and six) or odds (three, five, seven and nine), but odds were the preferred choice. All players had a driver, so including a two wood meant that the player had two clubs hitting the ball similar distances. Today virtually all manufacturers have ranges that consist of a driver and three, five and seven woods, with an inch difference in length.

WOOD STANCE

Balance and control are just as essential when using a fairway wood as a driver, but the power and distance needed come from the club itself. A player needs to reduce slightly the width of the stance to around shoulder width, with the ball position farther back to ensure a clean hit.

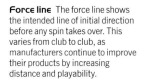

Force line The force line shows the intended line of initial direction before any spin takes over. This varies from club to club, as manufacturers continue to improve their products by increasing distance and playability.

Clubhead At impact, the clubhead should be at right angles to the target, with the ball striking the center of the face; the club should just brush the ground.

Hybrid Clubs

The hybrid club is a combination of a long iron and a fairway wood in both appearance and performance. It has less bulge behind the clubface than a wood but more bulge than a long iron.

Before hybrids, golfers tended to prefer fairway woods or long irons, but they now have the option of a hybrid. A hybrid's shaft is more like a long iron shaft in length, which gives more control, but the head design gives more height and playability. Constructed from steel, the heads are relatively small, and because the ball flight is lower than a fairway wood, this appeals to the better golfer.

Until recently, professionals generally had long irons in their bags, but now that adapted golf courses require differently flighted shots, it is not uncommon to see a pro with two or more fairway woods or one or two hybrid clubs. Even 10 years ago, almost all pros had the same selection of clubs—a driver, a three wood and irons, from either a one

Appeal The elegant shape and practicality of the hybrid make it very attractive to customers, who usually prefer to avoid long irons.

Inner weighting Because hybrids are designed to be less bulky than fairway woods but more forgiving than long irons, the internal weight cannot be as far back as in a wood but must be farther back than in an iron.

iron or two iron down through the set. Given the hybrid's rise in popularity, most manufacturers don't even make one irons now, and two irons are becoming rare.

When hybrid clubs were introduced into the market, they were largely avoided by the public because of their unusual shape. But as soon as the professionals began to use and promote them, amateurs gained the confidence to buy them.

TOE

During the swing at impact, the shaft bends and flattens the lie of the club, so the toe should be slightly raised at address in order to counterbalance this.

FACE

A hybrid's face is hollow in design to help players strike from the center.

SOLE

The sole of a hybrid is quite flat in design and short in width to help produce consistent striking patterns.

ADDRESS

Like any club, the leading edge should be at 90° to the target, with the correct loft showing.

51

HYBRID CLUBS

DESIGN

The club design determines how the shaft is secured into the head. Like drivers and fairway woods, some manufacturers prefer the through-bore method, where the shaft goes all the way through the head to the sole for added stability. Other companies choose the more conventional option of using a hosel for stability, with the shaft entering only around two thirds of the head.

Mizuno CLK Fli-Hi
This hybrid incorporates an ultralight titanium crown, which accounts for only 2.6 percent of the club's weight, allowing extra weight to be shifted lower to increase launch and improve forgiveness.

Ben Hogan CFT ti
An extremely low and deep center of gravity provides enhanced playability as well as excellent feel.

TaylorMade Burner Rescue The very shallow face on this club, which allows weight to be placed farther back and lower, makes a high launch possible.

Mizuno MX Fli-Hi
The benefits of this club include an increased sole thickness in the toe, to help with common mishit patterns, and added weight in the heel to enhance the draw shape.

Ping Rapture V2 A tungsten sole plate moves the center of gravity lower and farther back, and helps create the club's high launch and playability.

This is why companies spend millions of dollars marketing and advertising their products using names that golfers know—Tiger Woods, Ernie Els and Sergio Garcia, to name just a few. When these big names promote a product the golfing public is led to believe that if they use the same piece of equipment, they might be able to hit the ball in the same way.

HYBRID STANCE

A player's feet should be shoulder width apart, which provides enough balance without losing control. The ball position should be similar to when playing a long iron—just forward of center—helping create a shallow divot without excess spin.

Loft

Loft starts at 16° and can go up to 25°.

Shafts

For men, steel shafts are preferred. Ladies and seniors generally use graphite shafts, due to its reduction in weight.

Sole

The sole of a hybrid is very similar to that of a fairway wood but is smaller in size. It is played like a fairway wood; the ball is swept off the ground rather than hit very hard. The design of the club gives the ball all the height that is required.

Variations At first glance, all hybrids look very similar, but on a more detailed inspection, they have very slight differences, giving each one its own selling point and unique look.

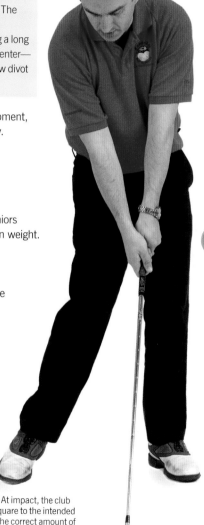

Clubhead At impact, the club should be square to the intended target with the correct amount of loft showing, enabling a player to produce the required ball flight.

Irons

A standard set of irons usually includes a three iron to a nine iron, though the set can include everything from a one iron to a sand wedge. Irons can be broken down into smaller sections: long irons, medium irons, short irons and wedges (see page 64).

The main consideration in iron construction is whether to choose a forged or a cast head. A forged head is made from mild steel. Low-handicap amateurs and professionals prefer it because the softer steel can be manipulated easily and it provides increased feel. However, it can also mark and damage easily. A cast head is made from much harder steel and is usually chosen by mid- to high-handicap golfers because it provides players with a larger sweet spot and helps with height and accuracy.

Forged design A forged head is constructed more for feel and appearance rather than to enhance a golfer's game—the majority of forged-club purchasers are already competent players.

Cast clubs A cast-iron head is usually constructed in three sections: face, head and sole. This speeds up the manufacturing process and creates a consistent product.

KEY FEATURES

TOE

More weight is directed behind the toe in a cast club than in a forged club in order to help reduce any twist caused by off-center hits.

FACE

The larger the face, the more room for error a player has, so game improvement irons have a much larger face than forged-blade or muscle-back designs.

SOLE

For ease of use, the sole is usually wider in a cast-iron club and weightier to lower the center of gravity and increase height.

BACK

This muscle-back design is made of forged steel for a soft feel, but has a small cavity to help correct the direction of mishit shots.

TOP EDGE

The top edge on a forged club is much thinner. A cavity-back iron is thicker, which gives the impression of it being easier to hit.

Long Irons

Long irons include one, two, three and four irons. The need for a one iron has almost disappeared, as hybrids and fairway woods are much easier to hit. Two irons are favored by some better players, but more and more golfers are instead turning to hybrids or fairway woods.

Many golfers today disregard all the long irons, and some players' sets begin at a five or six iron. This is due to the ease of the clubs, both in weight and design.

All manufacturers have their individual lofts, but an average one iron would have been around 16° or 17° in loft; a two iron, 20°; a three iron, 24° and a four iron, 28°.

In the past 10 years, however, as clubs have changed in design and become easier to hit higher, lofts have been revised. Modern lofts on three and four irons are now 2° stronger than before, reducing the need for one and two irons even more. Strengthening the loft of a one and two iron would create such a strong club that only the very strongest hitters would be able to get them airborne. They would also be extremely difficult to direct.

Long irons Long irons are renowned for being difficult to hit, but the larger sweet spot and lower center of gravity found on many modern editions makes them more playable.

4 iron 3 iron 2 iron

180 yds **190 yds** **200 yds**
(165 m) (174 m) (182 m)

An average golfer is expected to hit modern long irons—two, three and four irons—200 yards (182 m), 190 yards (174 m) and 180 yards (165 m) respectively. Long irons have a lower ball flight, which can be a huge benefit in the wind or if a low running shot is required on a hard fairway. This again shows why golfers tend to lean toward hybrids

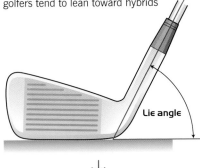

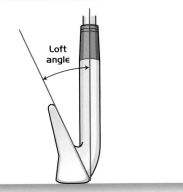

Angles Because long irons are obviously longer in length, the lie angle must be flatter to allow the club to address the ball correctly. The loft must also be set at an angle to help produce the correct ball flight.

Long iron distance Due to their lower ball flight, long iron distances can greatly increase if played on fast running type courses. Depending on the conditions, a well-struck two iron can roll up to 40 or 50 yards.

or fairway woods, as most courses have protection around the greens in the form of bunkers or water.

A low running shot is the worst type of shot into these greens, as the hazards collect many low shots, whereas a higher-flighted shot can carry all the trouble, land on the green and not roll off the back owing to the angle of its landing and the added backspin. However, on courses in Scotland or anywhere near the ocean, a low ball flight is perfect, as the wind changes accuracy and direction.

Clubs with long shafts are harder to control, so when hitting at a green with a long iron from a distance of up to 200 yards (182 m) or more, the expectations of a player are much lower because it is a difficult shot.

Shafts in irons should be matched. A player needs to get used to the weight and feel of his or her clubs, and most golfers admit that when changing their clubs, it can take weeks or months to get completely familiar with them. Professionals also have the same problem when changing irons, but they can hit thousands of practise balls and get used to a new set more quickly than the average golfer, who probably plays two or three times a month.

DESIGN

Iron heads are categorized into three main styles: blade, muscle-back and cavity-back. These designs have hundreds of variations.

A blade style is considered to have a very classic look with a simple, slim design. It is usually constructed of mild steel, and the weight is distributed fairly evenly throughout the clubhead. A good strike from the center of the club produces a powerful shot with a huge amount of feel. However, the sweet spot is very small, and any shot struck a fraction away from this point can lose a larger percentage of distance, so only highly competent players have the ability to use these clubs effectively.

A muscle-back club is also aimed at better players. It is constructed from mild steel and has a thin top edge. However, to help with playability, the back of the club has either a small cavity or a slight amount of added weight toward the toe and heel end of the head. This results in a slightly larger sweet spot and gives a player the same feel, but with some room for error.

Cavity-back irons, or game-improvement irons, are purpose built for the novice golfer who wants to boost his or her game. They are much larger in size, are constructed from harder steel and have a completely different look. Increasing the cavity and placing more weight around the perimeter of the back of the head maximizes the size of the sweet spot and makes the club much easier for players to use, especially those who can't always find the center. A cavity-back design allows manufacturers to put more weight in the sole to lower the center of gravity and create extra height. This, combined with a thicker top edge, leads to a club that is designed to improve an average golfer's shots and overall game.

Callaway X-22 Cavity This club's precise weight distribution provides greater forgiveness and stability, and the polycarbonate shaft tip helps dampen the vibrations, creating a softer feel.

Ben Hogan Apex Blade The chrome finish, thin sole and top edge give this club a classy, professional look.

Ping S57 Blade Constructed from stainless steel, this club has the look of a blade but the playability of a cavity.

Callaway Big Bertha Diablo Cavity This club has a wide sole for playability and a long heel-to-toe area, allowing the weight to be placed in certain areas for optimum distance and accuracy.

Mizuno MX-950 A mix of two hybrids (21° and 24°) directly replaces traditional three and four irons, with hollow-technology irons (five, six and seven) offering midset flight and distance and forged short irons (eight, nine and PW) providing precision and added feel in the short game.

TaylorMade Burner Cavity Inverted-cone technology expands the area on the clubface, delivering higher ball speed and more consistent distance from shot to shot.

Mizuno MP-67 Blade The muscle-back design helps achieve complete ball control by pinpointing the center of gravity. A neutral center of gravity (relative to the shaft axis) and a consistent sweet spot location allow quality ball strikers to work the ball in either direction while maintaining control of the trajectory.

Medium Irons

Medium irons are known as the five, six and seven irons. When golfers use these clubs, the expectations are increased. Because of the shorter length of the shaft and the increase in loft, they are easier to hit on target than long irons.

A golfer should expect distances of 170 yards (155 m), 160 yards (146 m) and 150 yards (137 m) from the five, six and seven

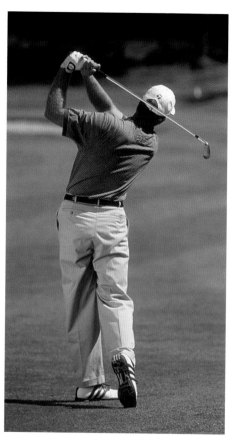

Medium iron play Retief Goosen sets the perfect example of how to play a medium iron by maintaining balance at all times and letting the club do its job.

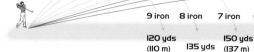

9 iron　8 iron　7 iron　6 iron　5 iron

120 yds (110 m)　135 yds (123 m)　150 yds (137 m)　160 yds (146 m)　170 yds (155 m)

Medium and short iron distances As the iron loft increases down through the set, the distances reduce, but the spin increases and the ball rolls less once it lands. This can sometimes take a while to learn but is vital to playing the game.

irons respectively. This leads back to the benefit of distance from the tee: If your tee shot is longer, hitting up to two or three clubs less into a green is very beneficial and can help lower your score.

It is crucial to have matching irons and matching shafts throughout your set. Since irons are the most used clubs in the bag, it is important to be completely confident with your clubs. Having your clubs custom fit is essential, but you also need to like the look of them. It might sound trivial, but being content over a shot helps a player relax, and this in turn helps him or her hit a better shot. Nevertheless, the clubs you choose must be beneficial to your game. For example, a 28-handicapper shouldn't buy a set of chrome-finished blades just because they look amazing.

Short Irons

Short irons are known as eight and nine irons and are deemed the "scoring clubs." When a player hits at a green with a short iron, he or she can attack the flag much more than when using a medium or long iron. This is because a completely different ball flight is produced.

An eight iron should be expected to travel 135 yards (123 m) and a nine iron, 120 yards (110 m). It is easier to hit shots that are loaded with spin with these clubs because short irons have extra loft.

Appearance A club's finish is dependent on its style. A cast club (left) is usually sandblasted, whereas a forged club (above) is coated in chrome.

With this extra spin—and increased control because of the shorter shaft—players can attack flags and stop the ball more quickly.

Furthermore, short irons provide a greater angle of attack. Because the shafts are shorter, a player's swing becomes naturally steeper. This creates a steeper angle of attack, causing the ball to roll up the face a millisecond longer than usual, producing extra spin.

This cannot be created when using long irons because they have the opposite effect: The shaft is much longer and the swing becomes flatter, creating a flatter angle of attack and producing less spin and a lower ball flight.

Better players who use clubhead speed to create a lot of spin can produce more controlled shots with both medium and short irons—this is how professionals can still attack flags from farther distances.

It is not uncommon for golfers to mix up their sets. Although not recommended, some golfers have long and medium irons in the form of cavity-back cast iron clubs, which have bigger sweet spots and are seen as confidence-building clubs because they are regarded as the easiest type to play.

The head design on short irons have a slightly deeper face, allowing the ball to roll farther up the face at impact because of the extra loft. This extra loft is very appealing to the eye and gives players more confidence.

Chipping

Short irons are also used for shorter chipping shots around the green. If a player needs to play a low running style of chip, he or she would use an eight or nine iron. The loft on these clubs makes them perfect for this type of shot—a five or six iron gives the ball momentum and keeps it low, but its longer shaft gives much less control of direction and power, even on a short chip shot. In addition, a chipping shot requires some lift, and a five or six iron generates very little height. The eight or nine iron works because it gives almost immediate height in the split second that is

IRON SETUP

As the clubs get shorter and more lofted, stance and ball position must change. The shorter shaft forces a player to bend over more, which produces a steeper swing, so the club is more likely to strike the ground earlier. Placing the ball farther back allows the club to be hit down into the back of the ball, producing the correct strike and spin.

required to get the ball out of the lie. Using a more lofted club for a chip, such as a sand wedge or a lob wedge, actually gives too much loft and very little forward momentum.

Spin

With the extra loft in short irons, the majority of spin created on the ball is backspin, and some established golfers like to move the ball in flight either from right to left or from left to right—otherwise known as a draw/hook or fade/slice for a right-handed player.

Having the ability to hit the ball in different ways is proof that your golf game is reaching the higher grade. To move the ball in the air like this, a player needs to put sidespin on the ball, which is almost impossible with short irons.

The smaller the loft on a club, the easier it is to put on sidespin, and this is why a three iron is much harder to hit straight than a nine iron. It is important to remember that if you are trying to hit a hook or a slice, you must use a less-lofted club.

Clubhead In all short iron shots, the club should strike the ball in a downward action to help create spin, with the ball hitting the center of the clubface at 90° to its intended target.

Wedges

During a round of golf, a player may use a wedge up to, or more than, 20 percent of the time. So, considering that a golf bag contains only 14 clubs, selecting the correct lofts for wedges is essential.

Around 10 years ago, players had up to three wedges in their bags:

- A pitching wedge had a loft of 52° and was expected to go around 110 yards (100 m).
- A sand wedge had a loft of 56° and went between 80–100 yards (73–91 m).
- A lob wedge had a loft of 60° and would be expected to go only around 60 yards.

Though the sand- and lob-wedge lofts have remained the same, the pitching wedge loft is now anywhere between 46° and 48°.

Customization The Ping Tour-W Wedge uses a tungsten toe weight, which ensures maximum forgiveness while maintaining feel with a custom tuning port.

Cleveland 588 60°
Cleveland 588 wedges are the industry benchmark for classic wedges. These tour-proven wedges have a traditional shape that promotes incredible touch around the greens.

Gap Wedge

The current pitching wedge has a maximum loft of 48°, so there is a large gap between it and the sand wedge. It is here that another club has been introduced. The gap wedge is anywhere between 51° and 53° and, as its name suggests, fits the gap between the pitching wedge and the sand wedge—basically replacing the old pitching wedge.

Hitting full shots with wedges creates the most spin. Though this is beneficial when attacking flags, players need to be aware that the natural flight of a wedge shot has very little forward momentum and a lot of height so any wind can almost stop it moving forward, knock the ball offline into the wind, and increase the ball's spin rate.

KEY FEATURES

TOE

A wedge is usually weighted more in the toe area to increase forgiveness and feel. A classic wedge tends to have a more rounded toe.

FACE

The face is much deeper in design owing to the extra loft and angle of attack. The ball rises farther up the face.

BACK

The back of a wedge depends on the club's design (blade or cavity-back). A blade design is more common—the milder steel promotes increased feel.

SOLE

Soles vary in thickness. The lie of the ball determines the wedge sole required. A thick sole is preferred for lush grass and a narrower sole for tighter lies.

DESIGN

The loft of the wedge and its grooves work together in harmony to produce the correct spin rate on the ball, allowing players to control the trajectory and roll on their shots. This is why manufacturers offer different lofts, varying from 46° and 64°.

Wedges can be bought in different types of materials depending on the feel required: forged-carbon steel wedges for a softer feel; firmer cast-stainless-steel wedges and clubs finished in chrome or soft nickel for a firmer feel.

TaylorMade ZTP Deep milled for their aggressive edges and increased volume, TaylorMade's Z grooves give their ZTP Smoke Wedge superior spin for greater stopping power on the greens.

Ben Hogan Sure Out
This wedge has a unique head design that places the majority of the weight in the sole behind the ball for extreme forgiveness and added bounce.

TaylorMade rac
rac wedges reduce the inconsistencies that are common in other wedge designs, allowing players to find their desired targets more often.

Mizuno MX Series Suitable for all players, MX-Series wedges have a triple-cut sole design and precision-forged grooves to maximize spin.

Ping Tour-W Wedge A popular choice with many amateurs and professionals due to its teardrop-head shape for ease of use from various lies and its small cavity aiding playability.

Ping i Wedge This wedge is designed with a concave sole and a tapered heel and toe that prevent digging.

Mizuno MP R Series This series features grain-flow forged wedges with amazing feel and a classic round head shape. They also have a tour-grind sole for ball control and consistent shots.

The type of lie is a huge factor in whether a clean strike can be achieved. Lie is always important in any shot but certainly more so around the greens. This is why wedges suit certain types of shots better than others.

Bounce angle The measurement in degrees from the front of a club's sole to the point that it rests on the ground at address is known as the bounce angle. The greater the difference between the rear of the sole and the front, the greater the bounce angle.

sole

As well as for full shots, wedges are mostly used for shots around the green, including:

- Pitching
- Bunker shots
- Lob shots
- Any shot less than 100 yards (91 m)

Pitching

Choosing which club to use when pitching onto the green is a precise process and requires a lot of practice to gain the necessary feel to be able to judge the distance, picture the shot and how to play it.

Pitching and the short game in general depend upon more practice than the long game. In the long game if a player hits an eight iron 140 yards (128 m) and is playing a par three that measures the same distance, assuming wind conditions, elevation, etc., do not affect the shot, the club selection is easy—an eight iron.

This rule doesn't apply as much when playing a pitch, as the player needs to imagine the shot and ask him or herself where to land the ball and how much roll is required after it lands. Since most greens aren't flat, the thought process needs to be like this: If the green is sloping away from you, the ball requires very little forward momentum. The slope makes the ball run, so a higher shot is needed because it lands softer than a lower shot. Alternatively, if the green is

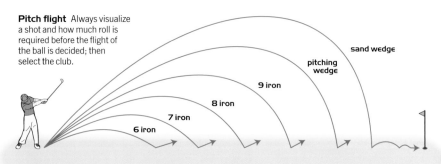

Pitch flight Always visualize a shot and how much roll is required before the flight of the ball is decided; then select the club.

6 iron 7 iron 8 iron 9 iron pitching wedge sand wedge

sloping toward you, a lower shot with much more run is required, as the slope would almost stop dead any high shot.

Na Yeon Choi Korean sensation Choi slides her sand wedge beautifully through the sand and maintains the clubface in an open position, taking advantage of the sole and bounce of the club.

Bunker Shots

It's also important to ask yourself this question: How much green is available? If the flag is located just past a bunker with very little room between the bunker and flag, this poses another problem.

The choice would be the most-lofted wedge—the 60° lob wedge—as the aim is to hit the ball high and with very little forward momentum. Unfortunately, when around the greens, the higher the ball is struck, the more difficult it is to control.

Lob Shots

Lob shots are a very risk-versus-reward type of shot—the reward is finishing close to the flag, but the risk is not playing a perfect shot and having to play the same type of shot again because the club went

Club grounding In bunkers, it is essential that the club is not grounded, as this incurs a two-stroke penalty.

too far under the ball. Another common mistake is to catch the ball too clean and whizz it over to the other side of the green.

Because there are so many options when chipping and pitching, it is important to practice different distances with different wedges, and to hit into soft greens as well as hard greens.

Grooves Always keep your wedge grooves clean and sharp to maximize spin and control.

Soles

Sand wedges are usually 56° in loft and have an unusually wide sole to assist the player when striking from the sand. This sole is designed in such a way that when the player strikes the sand, rather than digging into it, the sole actually bounces off the sand and does not actually strike the ball at all. It is the sand that causes the ball to come out and land softly.

This type of sole is also useful when hitting from soft lush grass, due to the same effect. A sharp sole just cuts through the soft turf, causing a fluffed shot. Alternatively, using a sand wedge with

a big sole causes trouble if playing from either a bunker with very little sand or on grass that is cut very short and tight. In these situations, a wedge with a narrow sole creates less bounce and enables the player to produce a sharper strike into the ball, giving him or her the required control. Creating a crisper, sharper strike allows the ball to have clean contact with the clubface and provides more grip as the grooves of the club create more spin.

Heads and Length

Throughout a set of irons the weighting is very consistent, and all the clubs feel the same. However, wedges have heavier heads, because the extra weight

Weight and feel Wedges feel much heavier than other irons, due to the added weight in the head. The additional weight aids players when striking through sand and thick or wet roughs.

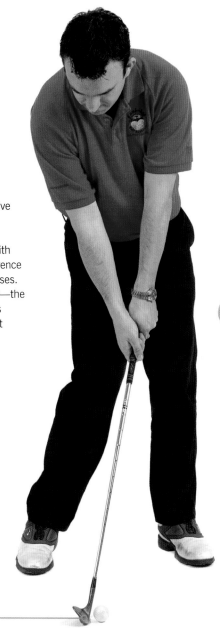

WEDGE SETUP

Because a wedge is the shortest of irons, it is important to be comfortable with the ball and allow yourself to bend enough. Placing the ball farther back in the stance ensures the correct strike. Having the ball in this position increases spin, which is desired for short wedge shots.

helps when playing bunker shots—although the club bounces off the sand, it still requires quite a lot of force to power through it. When pitching and with all short shots, it is imperative that the clubface accelerates through impact; a heavier head helps encourage this.

Finally, it's important to remember that with irons, there is half an inch (13 mm) less difference in length between each club as the loft increases. With wedges, the length reduces even further—the difference between the four wedges can be as little as half an inch (13 mm), though different manufacturers do have standard lengths.

Address position A sand wedge's wider sole usually produces more bounce, so when playing a shot from tight grass, a wedge with less bounce is a wiser option.

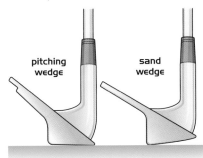

pitching wedge

sand wedge

Clubhead The clubhead should be square to the target, with the ball compressing on the face and rolling up it to create spin. A divot should always be produced owing to the angle of attack.

The Putter

Putting is the point where the game is arguably won or lost. Amazing ball strikes, long hits and great short games are everyone's dream, but decent scores are almost impossible without good putting.

The putter is the most used club in the bag. A novice golfer might expect to two-putt every green for 36 putts, while a tour professional would probably expect closer to 28 or 29 as an average putting round. Every round is different, however. Some days the novice player will roll everything in for 29 putts and the pro might miss almost everything for 35 putts. This is what makes putting so frustrating, but also so wonderful. A novice golfer could never regularly hit the ball 300 yards (274 m) into the air like a tour pro, but he or she could knock in a 30-foot (9-meter) putt just like a professional.

Putting brings everyone down to the same level and is based on two key points:

- Line and pace are the main considerations when studying a putt
- Without the right pace, the line is almost irrelevant; without the right line, the pace is also irrelevant

In the end, putting is all about feel and judgment. Technique, relatively speaking, almost takes a back seat.

Design

Manufacturers have created many different designs made from various materials to help the golfer hole putts. Some professionals use the same putter for years; others change every week.

Adjustable weights Because of the variation of green speeds on different courses, it is useful to have a putter with interchangeable weights to help maintain feel.

KEY FEATURES

FACE

A putter's face can vary from a smooth to a milled finish. The latter aids in feel and makes the ball roll earlier.

BACK

The cavity in the rear redistributes the weight closer to the heel and toe, and stops the face from twisting at an off-center strike.

ADDRESS

The marking on the rear of a putter helps players with alignment, ensuring that the face is 90° to the target.

SOLE

Various sole widths are available, but they are usually flat so that the putter sits flat at address.

DESIGN VARIATIONS

Putters have more variations in design than any other club, but a few types remain constant and have stood the test of time. These are the heel- and toe-weighted putters, which are regarded as industry standard in shape. Putters differ mainly in head and neck positioning and head material, and they can be altered to suit a player's desired look and feel.

Odyssey Black Series i 2 Ball This putter has an extended mallet head with a tungsten weight plug.

Ping Redwood ZB This putter is made from 303 stainless steel and is 100 percent milled for extra feel.

TaylorMade Rossa Core Classic Lambeau A 304 stainless steel construction with a Tuscan nickel finish provides a classic look.

Ping Craze-E One An aluminum head with tungsten weights occupies all four corners, providing maximum forgiveness.

TaylorMade Rossa Monza Spider Movable weights allow players to increase weight away from the face and help reduce twist.

Ping i-Series Half Craz-E
This putter is decreased in size from the Craz-E and has an easier alignment system.

TaylorMade Rossa TP Kia Ma Daytona This putter features custom tungsten weights in the back cavity for a deeper and lower center of gravity.

Mizuno Bettinardi BC5
Milled from a single carbon steel block, this putter also has additional face milling for ultimate feel.

Mizuno Bettinardi CO5 Identical to the BC5 in shape, a compact mallet and the plated satin pearl finish gives a classic look and feel.

Odyssey White Hot XG Hawk
A half-hex mallet head with an alignment line and weighted wings helps with stability.

Ping i-Series Craz-E
Sole inserts extend the weight to the perimeter, and a urethane insert is added for a soft feel.

Goal Although all putters look and feel different, their goal is the same: to put the ball in the hole.

No matter what, players need to do whatever helps them to hole a putt. If a player has a better feel, however, he or she is more likely to get the speed right, which is half the battle.

Putters were initially made to help the ball ping off the face, but as time passed, the experts realized that this made it more difficult to control. Putters with softer metals were introduced, along with putters with inserts that acted almost as a cushion to the ball.

As with iron technology, putter designers experimented with weight distribution in order to reduce the amount of twist in the head when the ball was struck off center. This is known as heel-toe weighting, where extra weight is placed at either end of the putter head to help stabilize it.

What makes putting more difficult is the amount of swing in the putt. If all greens were perfectly flat, all putts would be straight and easier to play. This is where the design of most putters can help, as many have alignment aids such as dots, a line or even circles. These are all beneficial to the alignment of the putter face and help when trying to produce a good putting stroke.

Pace

Achieving the correct pace and being able to read the greens are the next steps in becoming a better putter. A player might have the best putting stroke in the world and always hit the putt on the intended line with perfect pace, but if the line is wrong, the putts won't drop.

Length

Once a player is happy with the head of the putter, there are still a few remaining options to be considered. One option is the length. The industry standard is 35 inches (89 cm), but this can be altered to how the player stands in relation to the ball or how long their arms are.

Alignment Most putters have either lines or dots on the back, and these can dramatically improve a player's chances of lining up correctly.

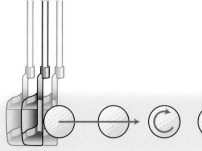

Roll As a putter strikes the ball it jumps slightly and slides on the grass. After this initial action, the ball then starts to roll, and the contours of the green take effect.

Grip

The grip on a putter is different than other clubs: the front of a putter's grip must be flat, unlike a circular grip on the rest of the set.

This flat front is perfect for placing both thumbs on, which helps keep the putter face square during the stroke. Grips can vary in size and are generally related to the size of the player's hands (see pages 110–111 and 180–181).

Styles

Players have realized that putting plays a big part in scoring, and manufacturers now cater for many different styles of putting.

HAND POSITION

Here are two variations of a putter grip. The key point is that both thumbs are placed in the center of the grip. Keeping the thumbs in this position reduces the amount of twist in the clubface. The most

important part of the grip is to maintain a firm wrist action, not allowing the wrists to "break down." This leads to loss of control of the clubhead and consequently loss of direction and power.

Takeaway The takeaway, or backswing, should remain short and firm. A takeaway that is too long can result in deceleration and too much wrist action.

Follow-through Like all golf shots, the clubhead should accelerate through impact, creating forward momentum. This is just as important during a putting stroke, as it promotes a smoother roll.

A putting style where the arms hang from the shoulders and the player rocks the shoulders to create power is the most commonly used. Players have recently begun to adopt other styles, including custom fitting putters with extremely long shafts of up to 50 inches (127 cm) or more in length and hinging the putter under the chin and allowing it to rock from side to side, with the chin acting as an anchor. Another variation is to have the putter rest on the player's chest or stomach and anchor it from there.

Ball Position

One of the main goals is to achieve the best roll possible on a putt, which is created by keeping the ball on the ground. Positioning the ball in the stance is key, as this determines how the ball reacts on the first five to 10 percent of its journey. Ideally, the ball needs to start rolling as soon as possible so that it remains on the intended line.

Positioning the ball just forward of center and just back from the left heel allows the putter to strike the ball very slightly on the up. This creates topspin and gets the ball rolling more quickly.

However, the ball does not roll immediately from the force of the putter. Even though the clubface is moving more slowly than in any other shot, the ball actually moves forward slightly in the air with no backspin or topspin; it's only when the ball is in contact with the ground that the spin and roll take affect.

Placing the ball too far back or forward in the stance creates a strike that causes the ball to bounce a few times, though it may not be that noticeable, before it eventually starts to roll. This in turn reduces its momentum and control, so that the player has to strike the ball harder just to get the required distance to the hole. Just like every other golf stroke, the more power required, the more control is lost.

SETUP

Creating a good roll on the ball is the key to successful putting. The main points to focus on at setup are:

- Ensure the head is over the ball so that a good arc is created.
- Place the ball slightly forward in the stance, which helps a player strike up on the ball and thus impart topspin earlier. This in turn makes the ball roll well.

Hips Keep the hips square to the target to allow the stroke to follow the correct line.

Knees Keep the knees square to the target at address to help align the rest of the body. They should also be slightly bent for added balance and comfort.

Clubhead Sit the clubhead flat on the ground behind the ball at 90° to the target with the correct loft showing.

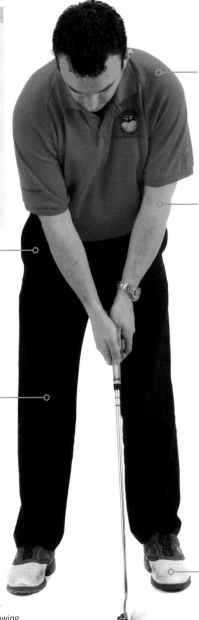

Shoulders A conventional grip makes a player's right shoulder slightly lower at address, but the shoulders should be square to the target to help promote a good line of stroke.

Arms Being relaxed in the arms helps control power. Don't give in to tension, but allow the arms to hang.

Feet Maintain a slightly narrower than shoulder width stance to help with balance, at 90° to the target to aid repeating a consistent stroke.

Club Maintenance

Clubs have developed over the years and are now made from steel, titanium and graphite. These materials make them much more resistant to both the weather and the beating they take from hitting so many golf balls.

The shelf life of a modern golf club is much longer than a club made from wood. Wooden heads require constant attention because the lacquer that coats the wood starts to crack and chip after several rounds of golf. The neck of a wooden club has a binding that comes undone occasionally and must be refastened, and the shaft rusts easily and needs to be kept dry. Finally, the leather grip dries out in the heat. Maintenance for modern clubs is much less stressful, but players should still take care of their equipment to preserve its

Shaft maintenance
Drying shafts with a cloth or towel after play reduces the chances of rusting.

use and resale value. One of the main ways clubs can be damaged are when they are still in the bag, especially longer clubs such as drivers and fairway woods. A bag carried either on the shoulders or on a cart gets knocked around, and it is extremely easy for clubs to get scratches on the paint or dented heads. This is why head covers are a good idea—they protect both the shaft and head from any potential damage. Iron covers are also available but are less practical, as the shafts are protected by the bag and the heads are solid, with either a chrome or sandblasted finish, so are more hardwearing. In addition, taking off and putting on a cover after every shot can become tedious.

Head maintenance
Through the continuous striking of golf balls, grooves can wear and heads can scratch and dent. Keeping moisture off the steel lengthens the life of the equipment.

Shafts
Shafts also need less maintenance. Steel shafts have a chrome finish, so after

play they require only a quick dusting with a cloth to remove any moisture, which can lead to rust damage.

Years ago, graphite shafts were sometimes damaged in golf bags; the dividers in the bags were plastic, and if a shaft rubbed against the plastic, it could be worn away and even weaken and break. Today, bags have protective dividers covered with a fake fur lining to stop any damage from occurring.

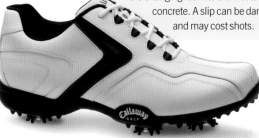

TIP

Maintaining equipment is a useful habit to get into, but another tip is to always check the studs on the soles of golf shoes. These wear away very quickly, especially if the walk from the changing room to the first tee is across concrete. A slip can be dangerous and may cost shots.

Grips

Grips are made from rubber, and though most should last a few years, they can dry out easily and become difficult to hold onto. In most cases, grips require a clean every 10 rounds or so, just to remove any dirt or grime and to keep them nice and tacky. Grips vary in terms of rubber, softness and thickness, so they may need to be replaced completely once part of the grip is worn.

Shaft protection Modern golf bags have built-in shaft protectors, and the soft fur lining stops the shafts from rubbing against the bag and weakening.

Head protection Placing head covers on woods and irons protects them while they are in the bag, where they tend to bang against one another.

Equipment Variations

Golfers usually have a general idea about the equipment they like and dislike in terms of look, feel and weight, but this is often based on very little information about each specific part of the club. Every club has hundreds of different potential variations, and rather than being influenced by friends or slick advertising, it is important to spend time finding the perfect clubs for you

The perfect club Putters, like all clubs, come in any number of styles and colors these days. Many of the variations serve more than a purely cosmetic purpose, with even the design of the face affecting feel and the putting stroke.

Product Cycle

The one thing that golfers now have more of is choice. Golf has expanded globally, and millions are spent worldwide on clubs. This means that golf manufacturers also spend millions on design and marketing.

Ten years ago, manufacturers usually introduced a new set of irons every three or four years. This has now halved to two years, and some companies launch new models as often as every 18 months. Drivers are the fastest-moving market. Previously, manufacturers launched drivers every two or three years. It is now common for a new driver to be launched every year, due to the sheer number of golfers. Manufacturers want a slice of the golf "cake," and this is why there is now so much choice in the golf club industry.

It is important to know the options available and to use these options to your advantage. The purpose of every driver is the same: to provide distance with accuracy. This applies to every club in the set—fairway woods, hybrids, irons, wedges and putters.

This doesn't mean that most of the equipment out there is somehow wrong; it simply proves the point that just like a player's golf swing, everyone is different and has different tastes.

Size and Ability

The majority of choices are influenced by the size and ability of the player in question. For example, a bigger, stronger man may prefer a heavier club so that he can strike at the ball with more force and have more control. Alternatively, a smaller person probably can't handle a heavy shaft or clubhead and is more likely to choose something lighter.

Look

Lower-handicap players are more likely to choose irons that have the classic look—a bladed style—which was preferred by the

Current models Such is the speed of change in the golf industry that it is not uncommon for manufacturers to launch a new or improved product every season.

WHAT IS A CAVITY-BACK?

Cavity-back refers to an iron that has its weight distributed around the edges of the clubhead, leading to a lower center of gravity and more forgiveness on off-center shots. It can also be referred to as perimeter weighting. Perimeter weighting enlarges the sweet spot.

Playability Even tour-spec irons use the benefits of additional weighting to improve playability.

top pros before the huge influx of cavity-back and perimeter-weighted clubs.

Cavity-back clubs are considered more appealing to good amateurs and professionals because their design makes it easier to move the ball in the air—something that only better players have the ability to do. The larger heads on modern cavity-back irons are much more attractive to the novice player, as they look inviting and appear to have more loft because of their design.

There is no exact rule when purchasing equipment, but with the introduction of custom fitting, a player now has the ability to acquire more information and thus make better decisions.

Variations Many manufacturers produce more than one model of a club, so it is important to look at as many options as possible.

Materials

Every golf club is divided into three sections—head, shaft and grip—and there is a choice of material for each of these.

Heads

A decade ago, most drivers were steel-headed. Today's drivers are either titanium or a titanium/graphite composite. Many manufacturers will produce more than one style of driver, and it's likely that the two options are available with most companies.

Fairway wood heads are usually made from steel, due to the cost and the unnecessary need to produce them with larger heads.

Iron heads are mostly steel, titanium or even aluminum. The few companies that produce irons with titanium heads do so at an extremely high cost. Some will use part steel and part titanium and put the titanium on the face, using the strength of titanium as a selling point. Any iron made from aluminum will have a short life span, as the material is very weak and cannot withstand continual use. But at a fraction of the price, aluminum does provide a low-cost option for beginners. Steel iron heads vary, and whether

they are forged or cast will determine the quality and type of steel used.

Over the years, wedges have had a large variety of different steels used to increase feel and spin, the two main ingredients for a good wedge. Forged steel, copper, chrome, gunmetal and rust finish are some of the different materials and finishes available in today's wedges.

Ping putters are the best known putters around the world and have a vast choice of materials available. Steel, copper, titanium and tungsten are just a selection of metals used when manufacturing putters.

Finish Woods usually have a painted finish, excluding the face, which helps reduce glare. However, irons are much narrower so glare is not an issue. Instead, irons tend to have either a shiny chrome or a duller satin finish. Softer, milder steel is coated with chrome for a more classic look, which appeals to the better players. Cavity-back game-improvement clubs tend to be made from harder steel and have a satin finish.

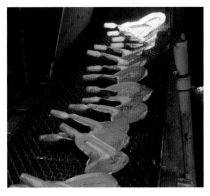

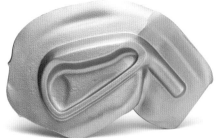

Forged irons The forging process is a long and expensive one, but the benefits are many. The result is an iron that has been created from a single piece of steel, without any joining parts, which increases strength.

Shafts

For most drivers and fairways the shaft material is usually graphite, though some players still use steel shafts. However, this option isn't recommended, as steel adds extra weight.

Irons, wedges and putters are mostly made of steel. Graphite shafts are also available, and weaker players usually lean toward this option.

Grips

Most modern grips are made of rubber. Though leather grips are still available, they are double the cost and have half the durability. With such a vast choice of grips, most manufacturers will have three or four grip options, but if a player finds a more specific grip, it is likely the manufacturer will send the clubs ungripped to allow him or her to have another style fitted.

The size of grips is always a consideration, and companies will have options related to thickness. For example, small hands require thinner grips and big hands, thicker grips.

Grips are usually available in ladies', men's, midsize and jumbo sizes, and if only a slight alteration is required, extra tape is placed under the grip to help thicken it. Alternatively, grips can be stretched slightly when being applied in order to make them thinner. This is sometimes used if a man has small hands, but doesn't want to use ladies' grips because of their color scheme.

Loft

Loft Though the difference in loft between each club in a set is only 3° or 4°, it is clearly visible, as this picture of a set shows.

Loft determines how far and high a ball will go and is therefore a key consideration for all clubs, including putters. Each club in the bag has a slightly different degree of loft, so it is important to familiarize yourself with them all so that you know which one to use in different game situations.

Loft has a huge effect on spin. Increasing it allows the ball to roll further up the clubface, thus creating more spin. Spin can also be controlled by swinging the club at different speeds, but this is difficult to achieve consistently. Altering lofts to suit a game is a much less complex way of getting the best from shots.

Drivers can vary from 7° to 13°, depending on the club speed and launch angle. Stronger hitters don't require as much loft, whereas slower swing speeds need the loft for height and distance.

WHAT IS "LOFT"?

Loft is the degree of angle at which the clubhead is set and is one of the deciding factors in how far and high the ball will go. The more loft, the higher the flight of the ball and the shorter the distance it will travel. The majority of woods and irons are labeled with a standard number (see "Standard Loft Numbers," opposite). The higher the number, the higher the loft, which gives the ball a higher and shorter trajectory. The lower the number, the less degree of loft on the clubface, which means that the ball will travel farther and lower.

Loft on fairway woods also varies considerably. A three wood can be as strong as 13° and may go up to 16°. This again is based on swing speed, but is also related to what the player requires. A player may require only one fairway wood, for example, so a 16° may fit the gap perfectly. If a player has a 12° driver, a 13° three wood is useless because the two clubs will travel almost the same distance.

Irons tend to vary less, as players choose models based on their ball-flight

Driver loft Though both heads are drivers, they have different lofts—one is 12° and the other is 9°.

Measuring loft The amount of loft on a club can be easily checked. The loft on a wood is unlikely to change from its original design, but irons made from softer steel can move over a period of time and should be checked annually.

requirements. Lofts can be adjusted, normally 2° either way. However, this is seen as quite drastic and is used only in cases where the player either hits the ball extremely high or low.

STANDARD LOFT NUMBERS

Driver	10.5°	6 iron	29°
3 wood	15°	7 iron	33°
5 wood	18°	8 iron	37°
7 wood	21°	9 iron	41°
Hybrid clubs (also rescue clubs)	16°–26°	PW (pitching wedge)	45°
2 iron	17°	GW (gap wedge)	48°–52°
3 iron	20°	SW (sand wedge)	54°–58°
4 iron	23°	LW (lob wedge)	60°–64°
5 iron	26°	Putter	2°–4°

Note Though these are standard lofts, they will vary between club manufacturers and models.

Wedges

Choosing the correct loft for a player's set of wedges is one of the most important decisions to make. Full shots need to be taken into account, but pitching and short games are even more important.

Having the right loft gap between each wedge is vital, and though 4° is known as the normal gap between wedges, some players choose otherwise. The most common modern selection is a 48° pitching wedge, a 52° gap wedge, a 56° sand wedge and a 60° lob wedge. However, a player may decide that he or she has room for only three wedges, due to an extra fairway or hybrid, and may need to alter from the suggested lofts above (still requiring a lob wedge).

This is where the options in different

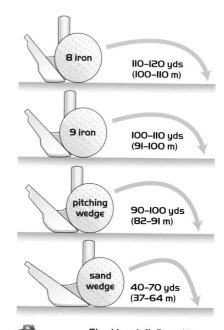

8 iron	110–120 yds (100–110 m)
9 iron	100–110 yds (91–100 m)
pitching wedge	90–100 yds (82–91 m)
sand wedge	40–70 yds (37–64 m)

Short iron loft Even with a constant swing speed, loft has a dramatic effect on ball flight. The more loft, the less forward momentum, but the more height and spin.

Width of stance Though the width of stance doesn't affect the actual loft of the club, a wider or narrower stance can affect the swing. A wider stance reduces the flex in the knees and makes the player very rigid; this reduces leg action and power. To counteract this, a player usually leans back at impact, increasing the club's loft and producing a weaker, flighted shot.

lofts are useful—the player could still have a 48° pitching wedge and also keep the 60° lob, but rather than having gap and sand wedges, he or she might include only a 54° sand wedge. This solves the problem of having room for only three wedges and also keeps an equal gap (6° as opposed to 4°).

Other players may try another method if they feel 6° is too much of a gap—a 49° pitching wedge, followed by a 53° or 54° gap wedge and then a 58° sand or lob wedge. This slightly reduces the gap in loft, but gives a little less loft at the very end of the set.

Putters

In contrast to popular belief, putters do have loft, and though not normally given as an option when purchasing them, there are reasons to have more or less loft. Before a putt is struck, it rests on the grass. Even though the grass on greens is generally very short, the weight of the ball still pushes down on it, making the ball sit in a very small depression. The loft on a putter instantly pops the ball from this depression, making it roll sooner. Manufacturers create different lofts on putters to sell in different parts of the

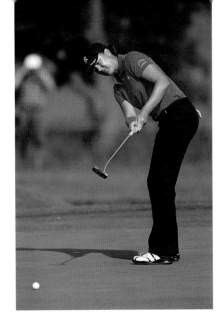

Putting A good roll is vital when putting, and the correct loft helps achieve this. Here, Sophie Gustafson of Sweden follows through her putting stroke.

world. The United States is known for very slick and fast greens, so manufacturers create the loft on putters for sale in the U.S. at around 2°. Europe has slower-paced greens with longer grass, so the ball sits in a larger depression that requires slightly more loft—usually 4°.

Too much loft on a putter makes the ball leave the ground too easily and for too long, losing control and distance. A putter with not enough loft doesn't get the ball out of its small depression and consequently starts jumping again, also losing control and distance.

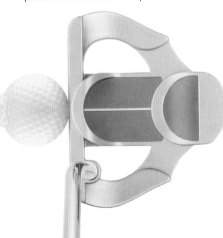

Putter loft At address, it may seem that a putter has no loft, but it can have anywhere between 2° and 6°. When setting up, try to see a small amount of loft on the face; this indicates that the head position is correct.

Weight

On a club, the two areas where weight can be felt and adjusted are the clubhead and the shaft. As they are mass produced, the head weights of drivers and fairway woods come as standard, but a large variety of shafts are available for these types of clubs, so a lighter or heavier feel can still be obtained.

Though each club model comes supplied with a standard swing weight, this is always adjustable when ordering. There is no exact science to whether a player should have heavier or lighter heads, besides the obvious: the heavier the head, the more difficult it is to swing. Stronger players therefore tend to choose heavier heads, and lighter heads are directed toward weaker players, helping them speed up the club at impact.

This is noticeable in the design of iron heads. Forged and muscle-back iron heads, which are usually aimed at better players, are 100 percent steel, so the weight in

Center of gravity (COG) The COG is defined by how far back it is from the face (A), how high above the sole (B) and how far from the shaft (C). Over the years, manufacturers have moved it around in an attempt to create optimum ball flight for greater distance.

Personal customizing Before the huge amount of options became available through custom fitting, some players would use lead tape to alter the COG in order to help manage their ball flight.

the head is fairly heavy. Companies that produce cavity-back clubs with perimeter weighting want to move the weight around to create the optimum hitting area—this is the reason most modern cavity clubs have different metals, graphite or even plastic located in the cavity. Heavier weight is placed in the areas that will be the most beneficial, and lighter metals, graphite or plastic inserted to reduce the club's weight.

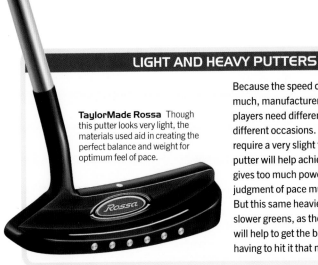

LIGHT AND HEAVY PUTTERS

TaylorMade Rossa Though this putter looks very light, the materials used aid in creating the perfect balance and weight for optimum feel of pace.

Because the speed of greens can vary so much, manufacturers have realized that players need different-weighted putters for different occasions. Extremely quick greens require a very slight touch, and a lighter putter will help achieve this; a heavy putter gives too much power and therefore make judgment of pace much more difficult. But this same heavier putter is perfect for slower greens, as the extra power produced will help to get the ball into the hole without having to hit it that much harder.

Wedges

Wedges are made heavier as a general standard, but players still like to have them suited to their liking. Though weights can be altered up and down, it is rare that players require lighter heads on their wedges. In fact, it is quite common for pros to want very heavy wedges. Steel shafts are very common in wedges; graphite is available, but most players choose it only to match up with the rest of the set.

Swing weight The swing weight states how heavy a club feels. The scale runs from A–G (most modern clubs are in the C–D range), with a number following each letter, to denote weight strength.

Putters

Putters, just like any other club in the bag, can be adjusted easily for weight, and some even have adjustable weights provided so that players can change the weight themselves (though this cannot be done during a round). By using different metals, putter manufacturers can produce identical styles with different weights and feels to suit any player. Though graphite shafts are available in putters, it is rare for golfers to choose this option, as this reduces weight. Most golfers have more problems leaving putts short, so the reduction in weight is more likely to enhance that fault.

EQUIPMENT VARIATIONS

93

WEIGHT

SWING WEIGHT COMPARISON

Iron	3	4	5	6	7	8	9	PW	AW	SW	LW
TaylorMade Burner Plus											
Loft	19°	22°	25°	28°	32°	36°	40°	45°	50°	55°	60°
Swing Weight	D2.5	D2.5	D2.5	D2.5	D2.5	D2.5	D2.5	D3.5	D3.5	D5	D6
TaylorMade r7											
Loft	20°	22°	25°	28°	32°	36°	40°	45°	50°	55°	60°
Swing Weight	D1.0	D1.0	D1.0	D1.0	D1.0	D1.0	D1.0	D2.0	D2.0	D4.0	D5.0

Look

When browsing through magazines, Web pages or in a retail outlet, a club needs to attract your attention. Following research, custom fitting and a trial, it may come down to a choice of two clubs. If both do the same thing and cost the same amount of money, which one do you buy? The more attractive club will usually win out, and this is why there is so much attention to detail in the design process.

Golf is known as a mentally tough sport and requires extreme amounts of concentration and confidence. Every player has experienced what can happen when concentration lapses or confidence slips. When playing a shot, if you like the look of your club, this will add confidence, which in turn gives you a better chance of a successful shot. The same applies to other areas of equipment, such as golf bags, shoes and gloves—they all do the same thing, yet they are available in all sorts of designs and colors. For example, titanium doesn't come in red, black or any other color; this is added at the end of the manufacturing process to make the clubhead more appealing.

Shafts

The same principle applies with club shafts. Initially, graphite shafts were manufactured in black so that people could tell the difference between steel and graphite, as steel was chromed and silver. But in the past 10 years, steel shafts have been produced in brighter colors to make them more appealing.

The biggest change has been with graphite shafts. A decade ago, nearly all graphite shafts were black. Nobody could

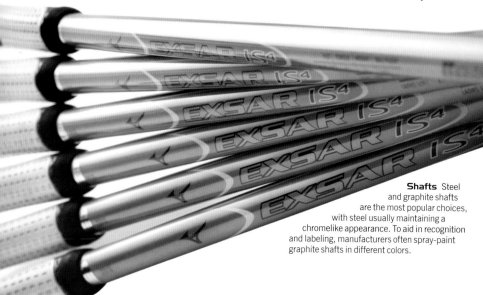

Shafts Steel and graphite shafts are the most popular choices, with steel usually maintaining a chromelike appearance. To aid in recognition and labeling, manufacturers often spray-paint graphite shafts in different colors.

identify any differences between shafts without looking very closely. Now, modern graphite shafts come in almost every color. With the huge rise in the number of people who watch golf on TV, manufacturers want their products instantly recognizable onscreen.

Putter variations The top putter shows a weight-adjustable design to aid in feel, whereas the bottom putter has an insert in the face to create extra feel.

Grips

Grip manufacturers have acted in a similar way. As recently as six or seven years ago, grips were generally all black, with perhaps some hint of color. These days, grips are a huge selling point, especially in retail outlets. When a player likes the look of a club, they will pick it up. The grip will provide the first impression of the club; if it feels right, and looks good, they will buy it with confidence.

Putters

The biggest variety throughout golf clubs occurs with putters. Drivers, fairways, hybrids, irons and wedges all have differences in look and feel, but nothing compared to the range of putters. However, because the putter is such an individual club, the look

is actually less important. If someone produced a putter that guaranteed to hole every time from six feet (2 m) or less but looked horrendous, it would still sell millions. This is because the average golfer has 36 putts, and it is possible to fall in love with a putter that can knock four or more shots off that score—there isn't another club in the bag that has that potential.

Grips Available in different types of rubber, each grip provides a different feel and amount of durability. The added coloring is purely cosmetic.

Feel

Feel is produced in a combination of ways. One involves the type of ball that is played. On a full shot, the ball compresses on the clubface for a split second, but in that time a vibration goes up the shaft and into the player's hands, which we know as feel. Though it is only a split second, we can recognize the differences in the ball used. If the ball is a two-piece core construction, this will feel much harder than a three-piece, which has a synthetic core and a much softer feel.

On shorter shots, the ball doesn't compress, so the feeling a player gets is from the outer cover; again, the type of ball has an effect on this feel. Distance-related balls have harder cores and thick, low-spinning covers. This means that the ball comes off the clubface a little quicker and with less feel, which can benefit higher handicappers who require extra distance on all shots. Lower-handicapped players and pros are more likely to choose a ball with a much thinner, softer cover to help provide the feel and spin they require when pitching and chipping.

Better players are usually those who need more feel from the ball and clubs because they have a more consistent strike—they have a better idea how the ball will react. A more novice golfer doesn't tend to strike the ball with as much consistency, so a higher-spinning ball that gives much more feel is not beneficial. Also, a loss of distance isn't an issue with a better golfer, but is more crucial to a novice.

Grip size The size of a grip easily affects the feel aspect. Anything too large or small removes almost all feel. Grips should relate to the size of a player's hands and the finger length.

Ball feel The softer a golf ball's construction, the more feel it provides. This is usually required for lower-handicap amateurs and professionals. A harder construction helps increase distance and is sought after by novice golfers.

Club Compatibility

Though ball covers and cores give players a variety of feel, if the club used isn't compatible, no benefit can be achieved. In relation to irons, forged steel will dampen the vibration caused by a shot and will decrease feel, whereas a much harder-cast head will feel almost like an explosion of the ball off the face. Using a hard ball with a forged steel is a strange combination, as the ball gives very little feel and the iron head enhances it, just as when using a cast head with a soft ball, no benefit is gained.

Feel is required more when the shot is shorter—for example, pitching, chipping and putting are classed as feel shots. A player who has the ability to get the ball close or in the hole with these shots would be said to have "great feel."

For all these short shots, the best players tend to prefer a soft-covered ball combined with wedges that are constructed of mild steel, and putters constructed of either mild steel or with inserts to create the same effect. Feel cannot be taught and is something that can be learned only through practice. This is when golfers who have previously played other sports such as tennis or squash can have a distinct advantage, as feel will have already been acquired.

Grip styles As the hands are the only parts of the body that come in contact with a club, they are the key to feel. When a ball is struck, the vibrations travel up the shaft directly to the hands. Gripping using the correct pressure and style dampens these vibrations. The two most common grip styles are interlock (bottom left) and overlap (bottom right). Players with smaller hands tend to prefer the interlock style for added stability.

Basic Club Fitting

There are many different aspects to consider when custom fitting as well as the initial requirements needed to begin this process. This chapter looks at the areas that are essential for a successful fitting, including players' static measurements and how they affect their equipment—with a particular emphasis on fitting drivers rather than irons. Iron fitting is covered in greater detail in chapter 5.

Custom fit Custom fitting was always considered "just for pros" in the past, but in reality the amateur golfer gains far more from custom fitting. It is worth the time and money.

Height

The height of a golfer has an impact on certain aspects of club fitting. Though it's not 100 percent accurate, it gives the fitter a good idea about how to proceed with the fitting.

The height of a player can dramatically alter the length and lie of the club, as well as the ability to produce power. It also gives the fitter an indication of swing plane. Though no records are noted, the fitter makes a mental note of the player's height and uses this as the fitting continues.

Height affects the swing plane, as taller people have to bend more to create a good strike on the ball. Shorter golfers using standard-length clubs normally find themselves farther away from the ball, resulting in a flatter plane of swing.

Before custom fitting was more commonly used, golfers bought standard-length and lie clubs and learned to adapt to them. Professionals were trained in the loft and lie areas of club fitting and altered their own clubs if necessary, and offered to do the same for friends and family members. When playing or coaching a golfer, if the golfer appeared very tall or short, the pro's natural instinct was to ask whether the player had his or her clubs shortened or lengthened.

Distance from Fingers to Floor

Though the actual height of a player provides an initial indication of potential club length, this doesn't take into consideration the distance from the golfer's fingertips to the floor. It is this important measurement that determines the need for any alteration.

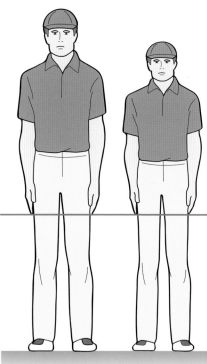

Club length Players' height and arm length can vary a great deal, so a tall player with long arms could need the same club length as a shorter player.

A very tall golfer might assume that he or she requires longer clubs, and in most instances this is true. However, if the player has especially long arms, longer clubs would increase the lack of proportion and makes him or her stand even taller and hit inconsistent shots.

Shaft length and lie A shaft that is the wrong length affects the club's lie at impact. The shorter the shaft, the more upright a club becomes; a long shaft flattens a club's lie.

too flat　　　**correct**　　　**too upright**

The same applies to smaller players. A reduction in shaft length isn't always the best option. Reducing a shaft's length minimizes the capacity for distance, and most golfers are reluctant to give up any length.

owing to the misleading measurements (as the golfer's fingers are wrapped around the club when gripping).

Custom Fitting

During this process, a player stands with his or her arms hanging by their sides. The fitter uses a measurement device to record the distance between the golfer's fingertips and the floor. This measurement registers on a chart indicating the necessary change, if any, in club length. Another benefit of seeing a professional is that the fitter can also analyze the player's setup stance and position at impact and recommend alterations.

Because the fitting process is so exact, there are always exceptions. For example, a player may be measured from fingertips to floor but may have extremely long fingers, perhaps an inch longer than average. This gives a slightly inaccurate reading

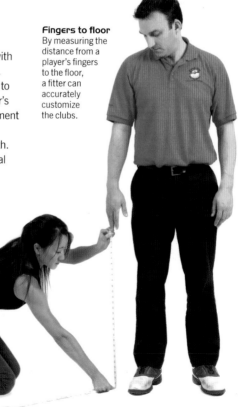

Fingers to floor By measuring the distance from a player's fingers to the floor, a fitter can accurately customize the clubs.

Swing Speed

A player's swing speed has a direct influence on how the ball flies. The more power created, the more spin produced, thus affecting the ball's flight.

A swing speed measurement records the speed of the clubhead as it strikes the ball. There are two main ways to do this. Most club professionals have a portable swing speed machine that is placed two or three feet (about 1 m) behind the ball in line with the target line. After each swing, the machine gives a readout of the player's swing speed. Following a series of shots, an average is displayed. This average speed is the information the fitter requires to ensure that the player has the correct flex.

WHAT IS FLEX?

Flex is the ability of a club shaft to bend as force is applied to it during a swing. If your flex doesn't match your swing speed, the clubface will not be aligned correctly, causing off-target shots. There are normally five ratings for shaft flex:
- Extra Stiff (X)
- Stiff (S)
- Regular (R)
- Senior (A, which stands for amateur)
- Ladies (L)

AVERAGE SWING SPEEDS

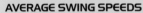

| Ladies—60 mph (97 kph) |
| Seniors—70 mph (113 kph) |
| High-handicap Men—80 mph (129 kph) |
| Lower-handicap Men—90 mph (145 kph) |
| Scratch Amateurs—100+ mph (161 kph) |

The more accurate machine is an indoor swing studio, which lets the player hit shots into a net while the launch monitor records various statistics, including swing speed. Again, an average is taken over approximately 10 shots to get a true reflection of the player's swing speed.

Shafts

The faster a player swings the club, the more clubhead speed is produced, and this creates more load or bend on the shaft. A stiffer shaft is required to help stabilize the head and give more control. Because of the kick in the shaft just before impact

Swing studio Many fitting centers have invested in indoor studios that can obtain all the required information for an effective fitting.

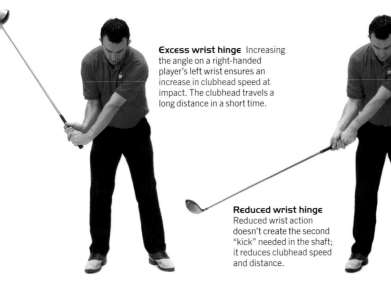

Excess wrist hinge Increasing the angle on a right-handed player's left wrist ensures an increase in clubhead speed at impact. The clubhead travels a long distance in a short time.

Reduced wrist hinge Reduced wrist action doesn't create the second "kick" needed in the shaft; it reduces clubhead speed and distance.

(see box below) it is extremely important to get the speed and shaft flex correct.

A player with a swing speed of 90 mph (145 kph) requires a stiff shaft. Anything softer in flex would bend too much at impact and cause the club to close and hook. Alternatively, a senior swinging at 70 mph (113 kph) using a stiff shaft wouldn't produce enough swing speed to get the club back square to the ball and would leave the clubface open,

resulting in a slice. Some touring professionals have swing speeds between 120–130 mph (193–209 kph). With such a load on the shaft, these players use the stiffest of shafts.

There are ways of increasing swing speed, such as giving a player a lighter shaft either in graphite or even light steel, but a player shouldn't attempt to swing as hard as possible. He or she should simply swing normally.

WHAT IS SHAFT KICK?

The shaft kicks in two areas:
1) As the player starts downsizing, the initial pull with the arms creates a bend in the shaft as the head remains still momentarily.
2) When the wrists unhinge just prior to impact, another kick in the shaft is created as the head tries to catch up with the hands.

Swing speed machines Around 20 years ago, these machines used high-speed video to capture a club's movement. Only top manufacturers purchased them, due to their high cost.

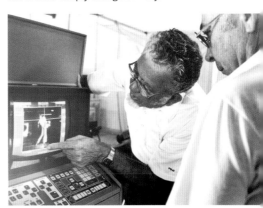

Launch Angle

The launch angle is the angle that the ball comes off the clubface. It is extremely important for distance, especially for driver fitting purposes. Once the swing speed has been decided, an optimum launch angle will give the most carry and distance. Too low a launch and the ball dips, losing distance, and too high a launch and the ball can balloon, with all the power pushing it upward rather than forward.

Together with the loft on the club, the height that the ball is teed at has an influence on the launch angle. By hitting balls into a swing studio with a launch monitor recording the results, a club fitter can analyze the results and recommend the correct loft. A ball that is teed too low is a common fault and causes its initial launch to be too low, resulting in either a low-flighted shot or one with

Creating launch Notice how Ernie Els' tee peg is still in the ground just after impact. This is evidence that the ball has been struck on the upswing, increasing launch.

high launch

mid launch

low launch

Tee height Altering the height of the tee and ball can dramatically affect the ball's launch and spin. The higher the ball is teed, the more likely the player will strike up on it, increasing the launch angle and reducing spin. The opposite occurs when the ball is teed lower. If the ball is teed too low, the launch is also very low. However, spin increases, and the result is a much weaker shot.

NO SHORT GAMES

The launch angle is considered a factor only on full shots and has no effect on shorter shots, as the benefit of a correct launch angle is to maximize distance. Any shot that doesn't require a full swing is not regarded as a distance shot.

too much spin. The shot will climb too high and lose distance as the excess spin will make it almost stall in flight.

When driving, the ball should be teed high enough so that at least 50 percent of the ball is showing when the club rests behind the ball at address. This encourages the player to hit up on the ball, creating a higher launch.

However, a tee is not used for iron shots. Here a particularly high or low launch angle can be successfully corrected by altering the loft of the clubs.

Loft

The actual angle of the launch and the flight of the ball changes depending on the loft of the club. For example, if a player's optimum launch angle for his or her driver is 15°, this will not be the same desired

angle for his or her five iron. Shorter irons fly the ball higher due to their increased loft and launch angle, which makes them a better choice for attacking flags. The driver will have a much lower launch with less spin, creating maximum potential distance.

Physically, a launch angle can change through the shape of a player's swing. A golfer with a steep swing automatically creates a steep angle of attack, which results in a higher launch angle. Alternatively, a much flatter swing causes the ball to launch significantly lower.

Pre-titanium head launch angle A low launch angle and a low tee height was more common on wooden-headed drivers because of their much smaller heads.

Ability

As a fitting takes place, the fitter looks for averages. A player who hits his or her first two drives straight and long might seem promising, but if the following six or seven slice off, the player's average will be in trouble. This is where the ability of the golfer is key. For a better player, it is much more likely that an average will be found after only five or six shots because of the more consistent striking. A more novice golfer is bound to have a few mishits, and these shouldn't be included in the average.

There are hundreds of potential fitting options—loft, lie shaft, and so on—so the more information the fitter has, the better. Knowing that a golfer is a five handicap or a 20 handicap early on helps the fitter prepare clubs for the fitting. For example, regular shafts with cavity-back heads would be aimed at an average player, and stiff shafts with muscle-back irons would be recommended for lower-handicapped amateurs and pros.

Time The more balls a club fitter sees a player hit, the more familiar he or she becomes with the player's ability. The extra time involved improves the fitter's service.

For a driver fitting, the better player would almost certainly require a stiff graphite shaft, with a high possibility of a loft between 9° and 10°. This might not always be the case, but by having these clubs ready, the fitter can plan ahead and help the golfer succeed.

Ability doesn't make the fitting any more or less effective. In reality, a higher-handicapped player is more likely to improve his or her game after a custom-fitting session. A low-handicapped amateur or professional is able to adapt to differences in clubs. For instance, if a professional is given clubs that are too short, the initial few shots would probably be too thin, but after 15 or 20 shots, the pro would have adapted him- or herself to suit the club. Higher-handicapped amateurs have less feel for their swing and are less able to do this, so amateurs often instantly benefit from a fitting.

Score A player's score is a strong indication of his or her ability. Keeping a scorecard is a good idea, especially if a player doesn't have a handicap.

Natural talent Even at the age of 13, Tiger Woods had impeccable balance and an elegant swing.

Ball Flight

How a player flights the ball can sway a fitter's choice toward any final adjustments that might be necessary. Along with using a launch monitor to calculate a player's swing speed and correct loft, a player will sometimes hit some balls on a range so the fitter can watch the ball in flight.

Though a launch monitor's readouts are accurate, hitting balls into a net doesn't always satisfy the customer or fitter; it is simply a way to double-check that the choices made are correct.

On a range, a player may find that the ball is slightly fading or drawing, or flying a little lower or higher than he or she wants. For example, if a golfer plays on a course that is extremely windy on most days, the player may want the ball to fly a little lower than suggested.

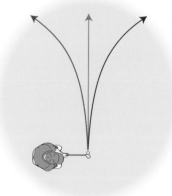

Ball direction If a player's swing path is correct, the ball starts on the intended target, but the effect of the clubface can still make the ball deviate, as shown above.

Power David Toms unwinds into a drive, producing full power and optimum ball flight. The ball has been teed high, encouraging an upward attack.

If a player has a little too much shape on the ball, either slicing or hooking, the face might not be returning square—even though the shaft may be correct for the swing speed. Besides lessons, the fitter may need to make an adjustment to help the player. This could be done in several ways. A lighter shaft would enable the player to roll the club closed a little easier (i.e. rotate the hands and wrists through the impact position to cause the club to go from an open face before impact to a square position at impact, then closed after impact), while a slightly thinner grip would also give the player

Visualizing the shot Carly Booth looks to start the ball to the right of the water hazard and draw it into the fairway.

quicker hand action. A shaft that has a stiffer tip would help stabilize the head.

Golfers feel happier knowing that the professional fitter has seen a ball fly, and not just a lot of numbers on a screen. This gives the player confidence that the fitting has been successful.

Ball flight A combination of launch, loft and spin gives each club a different flight. Understanding these flights and using them correctly can improve a player's performance.

Hand Size

The hands are the only parts of the body that are in contact with the club, and they have complete control over the clubface. Hand size has a big influence on a golfer's control and grip.

Grip size A player with large hands or long fingers is likely to need bigger grips in order to hold the club with the correct feel and tension.

In general, the larger a golfer's grip is in diameter, the less active the hands are. This can be an advantage or a hindrance depending on the player's normal shot shape. A right-handed player who fades the ball in the air from left to right doesn't benefit from very thick grips, as the club is required to be square to the target at impact in order to create the correct spin to make the ball fly straight. Because the hands have the job of closing the clubface at impact, thicker grips make this even more difficult.

The opposite happens if a player hits the ball from right to left and has thinner grips—the hand action becomes more active and is more likely to close the clubface, increasing the severity of the hook.

Types of Grip
Hand size also has an effect on the type of grip that a player uses. The two most common styles of grip are an interlock grip and an overlap grip.

With an interlock grip, only six fingers hold onto the grip, and the little finger of the right hand interlocks with the index finger of the left hand, almost binding the hands together. This style of grip is slightly less preferred than the overlap grip and is more recommended to golfers who have smaller hands.

The overlap grip is very similar, but has seven fingers holding the grip, and rather than the right hand's little finger interlocking, it overlaps the index finger of the left hand—hence the name.

Grip Size
How the actual grip fits inside the player's palm is important. Though ball flight can affect grip size, a player will struggle to hold on with a grip that is too large or too small.

Hand size Hands vary in size, so a snug-fitting glove and correct-size grip are essential to obtaining feel.

Jack Nicklaus Jack Nicklaus' small hands required slightly thinner grips, and he opted for the interlock grip. This gave him the control and feel needed to become a world champion.

PRESSURE

Grip size relates to the pressure the player applies. A grip that is too small creates less pressure, giving the player much less control of the club. A grip that is too big creates too much tension and a tightening of the forearm muscles, resulting in very little feel and control.

When a player holds a club, the fingers of the left hand should wrap around the club, but only enough so that they rest against the fleshy part underneath the thumb. A grip that is too small causes the fingers to dig into the hand, and the player might loosen his or her grip. A grip that is too big produces a situation where the player cannot get his or her fingers around the grip, causing the player to hold too tight.

Seniors

Age The aging process hits everyone in the end. The body begins to restrict movement, resulting in less clubhead speed and power.

Playing golf eventually affects everyone the same way. As a player ages, the body becomes less supple and cannot rotate or turn as much. This is a perfect opportunity for a custom fit.

Though the term "seniors" refers to golfers who are aged 50 or older, many people still continue to play excellent golf into their later years, and custom-fitted equipment has a great deal to do with this.

If a player has had the same clubs for 10 years or so, he or she becomes very comfortable with them. However, over this period the player's swing may

Fitness Staying healthy and flexible is the key to maintaining your golfing ability. Tom Watson still strikes the ball as well as he did 30 years ago.

become a little shorter owing to less flexibility, which leads to a reduction in swing speed and a loss of distance.

Changes in Clubs

The common outcome after a fitting for a senior golfer is the application of more loft on his or her driver to counteract the reduction in swing speed and consequent loss of spin. A softer shaft flex might also complement the reduced strain on the shaft due to less clubhead speed. Irons are affected by similar changes in

Shortened backswing This is the typical position of a senior golfer—it is effective but lacks power. Modern equipment has helped dramatically; with the introduction of lighter heads and shafts, senior golfers can produce increased clubhead speed without putting in any extra physical effort.

loft and shaft flex. In addition, moving from steel to graphite irons is beneficial for seniors. Because graphite is lighter, it's much easier to create more clubhead speed without putting in any more effort.

Thanks to custom fitting, new club head designs that help with off-center hits and produce more height can improve or maintain a senior's golfing ability for many more years.

Juniors

When dealing with junior golfers, it is important to consider that their ability and swing control are likely to change in the near future. Most juniors are interested in hitting the ball as far as possible, and many have an overswing to help generate power because their wrists and forearms aren't yet fully developed.

The junior is likely to grow a significant amount in a short time, making the custom-fitting process very difficult. It is important when fitting juniors to allow for growth and a possible swing change.

Juniors tend to hit the ball very high, which is a reaction to overswinging and too much wrist action in the swing. As juniors develop into adult golfers, the muscles used in the swing strengthen and the backswing normally reduces in length, minimizing the amount of wrist action.

Short Game

Even in the short game, a junior's approach is different to that of an established golfer. Juniors have their sights only on holing

Junior sets Most manufacturers produce junior sets that usually consist of a driver, a fairway, a hybrid, an iron, a wedge and a putter. These sets are the perfect way to introduce an eager youngster to the game of golf.

Gregory Norman Son of the world-famous Greg Norman, Gregory shows the importance of balance even at a young age.

Fearless Not put off by the water, this seven-year-old blasts his shot over the hazard with no fear. This reckless approach usually subsides with age.

putts or chipping in. When playing a pitch, they prefer the more difficult lob shot to a lower pitching shot. And when faced with a difficult six-footer downhill, they don't consider the return putt and tend to strike these types of shots with extreme confidence. As golfers mature and play in different situations with various styles of courses and weather conditions, they learn that the high-risk option isn't always the best answer.

Ping junior set With the quality and look of adult clubs, this set makes juniors feel just like the top pros.

5

Detailed Custom Fitting

A detailed custom fitting consists of many
specific areas that need to be considered
to make the fitting a success. These factors
include the action of the ball, how the
clubface behaves at impact, and how
weight can influence the shape of
the shot and ball flight.

Open cart view Detailed custom fitting is not just about making
sure clubs are right for the player, but can expose any problems in
technique that may affect your game. Millions leave the game every year
because of consistently poor form and results; with proper analysis
of their game, any golfer can avoid that pitfall.

Why Go For Detailed?

A detailed custom fitting supplies the fitter with more information so they can choose equipment of most benefit to the player. It can also answer questions about why the player may be striking the ball inconsistently, losing distance or not hitting the ball straight.

In the past, a player may have been put off having a custom fitting for a set of irons, due to either the added cost or the time involved. In addition, some players felt they weren't good enough at the game to justify making any adjustments to their clubs. But, today, custom fitting is almost a necessity—if you don't have a fitting, it's akin to giving your opponents extra shots, making the game even more difficult than it already is.

Every golf retail outlet has a fitting center or a launch monitor—or the option to book a fitting directly with the manufacturer. Custom fitting has

Mizuno fitting center Many manufacturers now give players the option of visiting a fitting center in order to try out the entire spectrum of club specifications.

Computer readouts With the help of computers, players can see the results of all aspects of a fitting, including spin, launch and ball speed.

become part of the iron-buying process and is available to everyone. Because of this, all manufacturers offer this service at no extra cost. An iron fitting gives a player many different options on length, loft and lie, to name just a few areas that are taken into consideration.

If a player is just being fitted for a driver, however, a detailed fitting is probably unnecessary. In a detailed fitting, a lot of information is given about the clubface at impact and the lie of the club, which are both irrelevant to the ball flight of a driver as the driver doesn't strike the ground at impact.

Physical adjustments Once a fitting is complete, the manufacturer must make the necessary physical adjustments to the equipment.

Software Manufacturers use their own software programs for fittings. This Ping fitting screen gives an indication of ball flight and the club's impact position.

Clubface at Impact

Where the clubface points at impact determines the sidespin of the ball. Ideally, a player wants as little sidespin as possible and more backspin to give more control; thus, the clubface should be at right angles to the target at impact.

Technology has made club fitting much easier to carry out. The original launch monitors and fitting systems cost thousands of dollars, and only the top manufacturers were in a position to buy them. But like the first cell phones and laptops, they were very expensive until they were mass produced. Manufacturing costs fell, and these products then became more accessible to the public.

Weak position The player has released the club too early, causing it to overtake his hands too soon. The result is too much loft and a weaker flight.

Correct position At impact the face is square to the target with the correct loft.

Square, open and closed A few degrees either way can dramatically alter a ball's flight, affecting both direction and loft. The more closed a club is at impact, the lower the ball will fly, while spinning to the left.

Launch Monitors

Before the introduction of launch monitors, the only way to capture the clubface at impact was to use video, which worked only with high-powered cameras that had fast shutter speeds. This process was expensive and was one of the reasons club fitting wasn't as accessible 10 or more years ago.

A launch monitor captures the image of the club at impact and measures how many degrees the club is off square. This is done after several shots have created an average. Once an average has been determined, the fitter inspects the equipment being used and begins to get ideas on how to improve the clubhead.

Ideally, a clubface at impact should be square to the target and flush to the ground. This allows the club itself to remain square and gives the player a better chance of striking the center of the face, which creates the most power.

Open or Closed?

Because there are many different things that cause an open or closed clubface, the fitter must take into account everything previously monitored. If a clubface is closed at impact, the following need to be considered:

- The shaft flex could be too flexible, making the clubface close
- The player could have grips that are too small, causing the hands to move position and closing the club too soon

A clubface that closes too much at impact is actually not much of a problem, and is commonly seen in better players.

Once the clubface at impact position has been finalized, other aspects need to be taken into account before any final decisions or alterations can be made.

WHAT IS SLICE?

The slice, or fade, is the most common fault and occurs when the clubface is too open at impact. Though it's important a player has advice about equipment and club adjustment, sometimes learning how to swing the club more effectively is all that is required.

Lie of Club at Impact

The lie of the club at impact relates only to an iron shot. When the club strikes the ground, it should be flat, allowing it to remain on target and not twist. If a club is not flat on the ground at impact, it has an effect on ball flight.

All players swing clubs differently, and it is not a fault that the club has the wrong lie at impact: It simply means that an adjustment is needed.

Twist

An incorrect lie of the club at impact makes the club twist, causing it to close or open. If a club twists at impact, the ball spins in relation to the club's new direction. Any club that is too flat at impact causes the toe, rather than the entire sole of the club, to dig into the

HOW MANY DEGREES?

There are general lie-change parameters relating to the number of degrees clubs can move. Most manufacturers recommend 2° either way—any more can weaken the steel. Very occasionally, a player might request at a fitting further adjustment of clubs that have already been altered by up to 2°. This can be done, but the player has to take responsibility for any possible damage caused by the weakened steel.

ground. This in turn makes the heel of the club overtake the toe, as the toe is now lodged in the ground. As the heel overtakes the toe, the clubface opens, causing the ball to spin from left to right in the air. It also encourages a strike toward the heel, reducing power.

Alternatively, if the club is too upright at impact, it will cause the heel to dig into the ground. The toe will overtake the heel, creating a closed impact position. This will make the ball spin from right to left. With the club at this angle, the ball is much more likely to come off the toe, producing a weaker strike.

Lie angle Because adjustments are usually only 1° or 2°, the process needs to be precise, and requires the eye of a skilled club maker.

too flat   correct   too upright

Accuracy

Because the amount of degrees that a lie can be adjusted is variable, the recording needs to be accurate. The process of determining the lie at impact is done by placing tape on the sole of the club and the clubface. The player strikes balls off a plastic mat, ensuring that the mat itself is struck. By looking at the sole of the club after several shots, the lie at impact can be

Lie at impact Incorrect lie at impact causes the club to twist as it strikes the ground, leading to poor contact and direction control.

determined from the markings on the tape. In addition, because the tape is designed to mark easily, there will be markings on the face showing where the balls have struck. By using this method along with different club specifications, it doesn't take long to find the correct lie.

Through impact Achieving the correct lie allows the club to travel cleanly on its intended path, as demonstrated by Adam Scott.

Checking the lie Placing special tape on the sole of an iron and hitting shots off a plastic board allows a fitter to check whether or not the correct lie has been achieved.

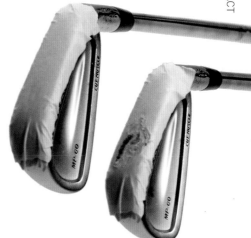

Spin

Spin rate is important during a fitting because it controls the ball's flight. Spin is created on every shot, and it shows how the ball reacts to the clubface.

When the word *spin* is used, people automatically think *backspin*. The amount of backspin produced can severely alter a ball's flight. With modern launch monitors, figures are collected so that any necessary adjustments can be made.

The faster the club travels into the ball, the more spin produced. Though backspin is very useful when trying to stop a ball on the green, it can also have adverse effects.

Loft

Applying too much spin makes the ball climb too much, resulting in a very high and weak shot. If this happens, alterations can be made to loft angles on clubs. There are other options for flighting the ball lower, such as using a different shaft, trying a lower-spinning ball or even swinging with less speed (though this isn't recommended, as clubhead

Loft and strike These are the two main factors affecting spin. The higher the loft and the cleaner the strike, the more spin will be created. Wedges produce the most spin.

WEDGES

Spin is generated by clubhead speed. On shorter shots, where the club isn't moving so fast, spin is very difficult to achieve. This is why wedges are always marketed as being high in spin. A good wedge provides a lot of spin, which in turn gives a player more control.

Pitching To maximize spin, a downward attack should be used. The length of the backswing determines distance, and firm wrists through impact keep the face from closing and maintain loft.

speed is so important and difficult to achieve). However, loft has the biggest impact.

Some players fly the ball extremely low and prefer not to change balls because of the feel. A softer shaft may help with height, but the player may then lose accuracy. Changing clubs to a model that is specifically designed to fly the ball higher is also an option, but again, the player may like his or her clubs the way they are and have no desire to change. The wants and needs of the player must always be considered. Altering one thing for the better may make another area worse. So, in the end, increasing loft might

WHY ARE GROOVES IMPORTANT?

The longer a ball stays on the face, the more the grooves can take effect. This is fine when playing a full swing shot, because the ball stays on the face longer. When playing a short pitch, this is not an option as the player generates as much spin as possible. The better the ball lies on the turf and the cleaner and sharper the grooves, the more likely it is that extra spin will be created. This allows a player to get a very clean strike into the back of the ball, almost squeezing the ball on the face and producing the extra required spin.

Angle of attack The steeper swing plane (on the left) automatically produces more spin, as the angle of attack on the ball is sharper. A flatter plane (right) creates less spin and a lower launch.

be the only option—that way, the feel, look and weight remain the same and the only change is a higher ball flight.

Altering lofts can be dangerous if we remember that there are only 4° between each iron. A loft alteration of 1° or 2° can have a huge effect on a ball's flight. Any adjustment in loft must be made throughout a complete set of irons; otherwise, gaps are formed.

Weight Distribution

When a club is designed—whether it is a driver, an iron or a putter—
no expense is spared on research into how and where to distribute the
weight for the best ball flights and the straightest shots.

The weight distribution is internal on drivers as the heads are hollow. Manufacturers experiment with placing different weights in various parts of the head so that they cannot be seen. Placing weights farther back in a driver's head brings the center of gravity farther back and lower, giving a higher launch off the clubface.

When it comes to iron designs, weight distribution also determines how a club will perform. Placing extra weight in certain areas behind the face can increase the sweet spot, making the club more effective.

Muscle-back Irons

A muscle-back, or bladed, iron has a very small sweet spot because the clubhead itself is smaller in size. In addition, the weight is evenly distributed throughout the head, making it extremely difficult to hit.

WHAT IS THE SWEET SPOT?

The sweet spot is the area of the clubface from where a player tries to strike his or her shot. A ball coming off the sweet spot gives the most distance and accuracy.

COG Moving the weight to different areas of a club can produce shots with different flights. The left shows a lower center of gravity (COG), leading to a higher launch angle. The right, the typical weight distribution for a bladed iron which produces a more penetrating flight.

Weighting Because drivers and woods are hollow, the weighting systems are usually done internally, but some manufacturers prefer to add weight externally—such as on the Ping Rapture V2.

Top amateurs and professionals have enough ability to use these styles of clubs, but as modern equipment becomes more commonly used, there are less and less of them available.

Before the introduction of modern cavity-back-weighted clubs, almost every golfer used a type of bladed club. It helps players if they understand the physics of weight distribution or get advice from a professional, so they know how to adjust the weight distribution to change the ball flight. Players can add strips of lead tape to areas on the back of the club, and this alters the weight distribution of the head. If a player finds that the ball is flying too low, a few strips of lead tape on the back of the club, placed lower down toward the sole, helps fly the ball higher.

Cavity-back Irons

A cavity-back iron's weight varies on the back of the club. Weight around the bottom, near the sole, helps with height by reducing the center of gravity. Having extra weight around the perimeter increases the sweet spot. This style of iron is usually made larger in size to aid confidence. The choice between irons and their

Putter weighting The key to successful putting is to reduce the amount of twist as the clubhead strikes the ball. Placing weight behind the face, usually toward the heel and toe areas, can reduce twist further.

weight distribution rests entirely with each individual player. Once a custom fitting has been completed, this is one of the last few decisions to make.

Putters

When dealing with weight distribution in putters, adding extra weight on either side of the sweet spot reduces the amount of twist in the head. This is why almost all models of putters have very little weight behind the face; more weight makes the ball travel off the face much too quickly and results in a loss of distance and control.

Muscle and cavity back Though muscle-back irons have a classic look, the cavity-back option gives more room for error.

Swing Weight

The swing weight of clubs varies. Players with slower swing speeds are likely to prefer a lighter swing weight so they can swing the club a little faster and create more clubhead speed. Better golfers with faster swings tend to have more control over their clubs so prefer a higher swing weight to enhance the feel.

The swing weight of a club is not its actual weight but how the club feels when it is swung. The closer the balance point is to the clubhead, the heavier the

SWING WEIGHT SCALE

Swing weight is expressed by a letter followed by a number—D2, for example. The scale is A–G in letters and 0–10 in numbers, and a combination of the two is known as a swing-weight point; there are 77 possible swing-weight points. Men's standard swing weight is between C10 and D1, depending on the manufacturer.

swing weight is, so that the club feels heavier when swung. Because golf is such a "feel" sport, it is extremely important to have a matching swing weight throughout a set of clubs; otherwise, a player might lose sense of feel.

The actual weight of a club is measured in grams. If a player adds lead tape to a club, its weight increases only by the weight of the lead, and this applies to any type of club. However, placing the lead tape on certain areas of the club does affect the swing weight.

Iron swing weight The swing weight of a set of irons is planned carefully. Short irons are always slightly heavier due to the reduction in shaft length.

A club's swing weight can be altered in only two ways: Up and down. If the swing weight needs to be increased, weight must be added closer to the head; usually on either the head itself or on the bottom of the shaft. To decrease the swing weight, weight must be added at the other end of the club; depending on the amount of lead needed, it can be placed either under the grip or inside the shaft.

Standard swing weight is fine for almost every amateur golfer, but as a player improves, he or she might notice that their sense of feel becomes more sensitive and the clubs may start to feel a little light in the hands. This is a signal that a swing-weight alteration may be required. Even if a player is happy with his or her clubs, simply trying a few irons with different swing weights can be a good idea.

Heavier clubs Tiger Woods swings at a tremendous speed and requires much heavier clubs than the average player. These clubs help control his power without the loss of feel. Slower swingers often find a lighter swing weight much more manageable.

Experiment Try out clubs with different weights to see how your game reacts to them. Be sure to seek advice from a professional—most have a large stock of trial irons to choose from, and some may improve distance and accuracy.

6

Swing

Golf swings have changed over the years, but the basics have remained the same. Top professionals need to have excellent fundamentals to produce their high-quality shots. Though their swings may look different, this is only because of height, size and the players' idiosyncrasies. This is where custom fitting can help—it can improve your game without altering your technique.

Ernie Els The natural swing of Ernie Els is considered the best on the circuit. For a player built more for rugby than golf, Els has an incredible lightness of touch and effortless grace.

Introduction to the Swing

Technically, if the fundamentals of the swing are correct, a player will produce good shots. However, achieving this requires lessons, time and lots and lots of practice. Most golfers want to play well but don't want to put in much effort, so swings vary from player to player. This is another reason why custom fitting is beneficial—it helps players with swing faults that might never go away on their own.

How a player swings the club determines many things, including:

- The impact position of the club
- The speed of the clubhead
- The shape of the shot

Players must imagine the ball on a line going toward the target. Because players must stand to the side of this line, this automatically makes the swing a rounded shape. The aim is to swing the club around the torso.

1 2 3

The Steps

Place the clubhead down behind the ball with the leading edge at right angles to the target line **(1)**. The body should be parallel to this line. Bending at the hips gives a player the correct posture to swing the club; this angle changes depending on the height of the golfer.

The next step is to turn **(2)**. First, backswing using the shoulders to twist 90° **(3** and **4)** until the spine is pointing at the target and the weight has shifted from being equally on both feet to the right side **(5)**. Then shift forward and unwind the backswing until the chest faces the target. Before, during and after impact, the hands and arms have a huge job to do.

On the backswing the wrists hinge to create 90° between the left arm and the shaft, which is released through impact when the body drives forward and accelerates. To achieve consistent striking, a player's posture should be maintained up to the point of impact, trailed by a balanced follow-through.

Balance

Rhythm and a consistent tempo are key to swinging the club the same way time after time. They also help with balance. All great players have good balance and a consistent swing tempo, though this varies from player to player. Padraig Harrington has a fast tempo, for example, Ernie Els has a much slower one and Tiger Woods's tempo is explosive.

4

5

Club at Impact

The position of the clubface at impact should replicate the address position. This is difficult to achieve, however—at impact, the club moves at a potential speed of 100 mph (160 kph).

Keeping the clubface square to the target line at impact ensures that the ball finishes at that point, and if the position is exactly the same as at address, the ball flight is correct in relation to the loft. But keeping the clubface square doesn't mean the ball travels in a straight line. Instead, it ensures that the ball lands at the target. Other factors, such as swing path, determine where the ball starts, and swing plane determines the launch angle and flight of the ball. The clubface decides where the ball finishes in relation to the target line.

During a backswing, the clubface is opened by a player's hand action. It is necessary to rotate the club around the body correctly and then close on the follow-through for the same reason. At impact, the clubface is in the process of closing, so it is very difficult to bring the club back square to the target. This is why top professionals spend hours and hours on the practice

range hitting thousands of balls—to perfect the action and its timing.

Grip

This leads back to one of the fundamentals of golf: grip. If the grip is incorrect, this affects the clubface during the swing, making it much more difficult to return it back square at impact.

Angle

Another reason for a clubface not returning square to the target relates to the downswing. If, during the downswing, a player releases the angle between the left arm and wrist too early, or indeed too late, the clubface is affected.

Ball strike Placing the sole flush to the ground is key to consistent ball striking. Striking the center of the clubface is also important.

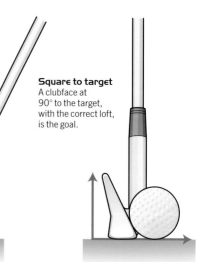

Square to target
A clubface at 90° to the target, with the correct loft, is the goal.

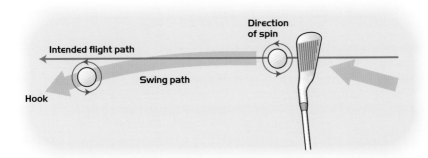

Direction
of spin

Intended flight path

Swing path

Hook

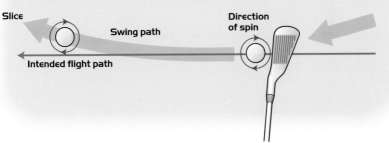

Slice

Swing path

Direction
of spin

Intended flight path

A release too soon brings the club down into the ball earlier than it should and is known as an early hit. This leads to several things, to include hitting the ground before the ball and closing the clubface too soon. If a strike is managed, the shot usually lacks in power, as more loft is shown to the ball. If this angle is delayed too long, it is known as a late hit and the opposite happens—a too-clean strike, an open clubface at impact and a lower ball flight.

There are occasions when a player perfectly returns the club back to the ball, but still hits the ball off line. If this occurs, the player needs to check additional fundamentals, such as alignment of both the clubface at address and his

Clubface in relation to target The position of the clubface relative to the target line indicates where the ball will finish, while the swing path gives the ball its initial direction. For a right-handed golfer, a hook occurs when a ball bends violently to the left, usually resulting in it finishing to the left of the target. A slice is the opposite—the ball spins to the right in the air, finishing to the right of the intended target.

or her body. Any clubface that points to the right of the target line causes the ball to spin to the right. How much it spins depends on the severity of the face and the speed at which it is traveling. These types of shots usually fly slightly higher because as a club opens, it adds loft. Any ball moving from right to left in the air results in a club that is closed to the target line at impact. Depending on the severity, the ball flies lower.

Shape of Swing

A player's swing shape is also known as the plane of swing. This is generally determined by the height of the player and the player's spine angle. A taller person has to bend over more for the club to rest on the ground, giving him or her a more severe angle on the spine, just as a shorter person has to bend less for the club to reach the ground.

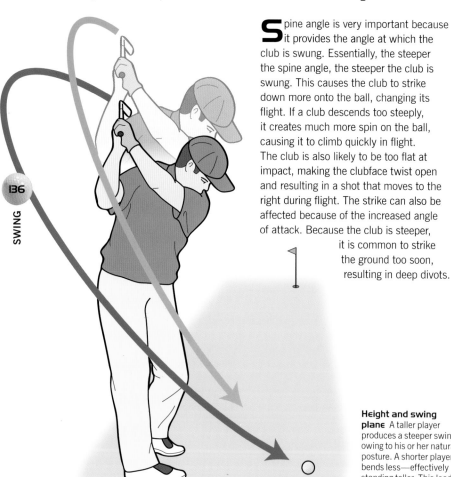

Spine angle is very important because it provides the angle at which the club is swung. Essentially, the steeper the spine angle, the steeper the club is swung. This causes the club to strike down more onto the ball, changing its flight. If a club descends too steeply, it creates much more spin on the ball, causing it to climb quickly in flight. The club is also likely to be too flat at impact, making the clubface twist open and resulting in a shot that moves to the right during flight. The strike can also be affected because of the increased angle of attack. Because the club is steeper, it is common to strike the ground too soon, resulting in deep divots.

Height and swing plane A taller player produces a steeper swing owing to his or her natural posture. A shorter player bends less—effectively standing taller. This leads to a flatter swing plane.

Bad Habits

Incorrect posture is not the only thing that affects the swing negatively. Players control the swing itself, and bad habits are easy to slip into. Many golfers unknowingly try to correct a ball fault by aiming farther left to allow for spin, taking the ball to the right. This is not a good idea: Aiming farther left opens up both the stance and the body even more, and the likely outcome is to produce an even steeper swing. Another action that can potentially wreck a swing involves placing the ball too far back in the stance to avoid heavy shots.

Michelle Wie Being very tall, at six feet one inch, Michelle Wie naturally produces a very steep swing plane. Her athleticism, flexibility and ability have made her one of the most powerful female golfers.

Posture and swing Correct posture puts a club in the right position at the top of a swing. Maintaining height throughout the downswing provides consistent striking.

This gives the player less time to use the hands to square the clubface, however, resulting in additional sidespin.

Similarly, if the swing plane is too flat, the club comes into the ball at a shallow angle, which is more likely to cause a thin shot. Because the club never gets a chance to reach the bottom of the ball, a lower ball flight is produced. And because the swing is flat, more wrist action is used during the backswing to enable the club to get around the flat spine angle. This can result in too much wrist action at impact, causing the clubface to close and a ball flight that moves to the left.

Moving back to the basics, if the posture is set correctly by tilting from the hips and then swinging around the spine angle, this automatically returns the club to the correct position. Along with your tempo and making sure the club and all parts of your body return to the right place at the right time, the important thing to remember is that if the ball does not launch off on the intended target line, there is a fault with your swing.

Downswing

The shape of the downswing usually mirrors the backswing, though this isn't

Steep swing A steep swing increases spin and creates a higher ball flight. It also produces deep divots.

always the case. A player may have a very flat backswing but a steep downswing, or a steep backswing moving into a flat downswing. This is not uncommon and is the cause of most slices.

By altering the downswing into a steeper angle, a player begins hitting across him- or herself. This does two things. First, the ball starts left of the intended target. Second, because the player's hands are much closer to the body, it doesn't leave enough room for the player to rotate the wrists square to the clubface, resulting in left-to-right spin. Players who change the downswing into a flatter plane tend to be slighter better golfers. This movement, if only slight, can help a player move the ball from right to left in the air, which is considered a better shape. This is fine, but extremes

Flat swing A flat swing reduces spin and creates a lower ball flight. It also produces a cleaner strike.

in both cases can result in a complete loss of control, accuracy and timing.

The likelihood of finding two players who swing a club identically is so unrealistic that golfers should put the concept of swing into perspective. Perfecting the swing will probably never be achieved. Timing always plays a huge part, and because the swing lasts only around two seconds, the chances of repeating the same swing time after time is almost impossible. Even Tiger Woods, who has achieved incredible success for more than a decade, has admitted to hitting only three or four shots—ever—that he considers perfect.

Swing Pattern

Though swings are never identical, patterns do emerge, and certain faults at the address position are likely to lead to other faults in swing movements. This again takes us back to golf fundamentals and the importance of being set up correctly.

Grip

A neutral grip helps the player to ensure the clubface is square at impact. A strong grip is defined by a player who has his or her hands too far to the right of the grip, which is more likely to produce a strong shot (low and hooked). A weak grip is when the hands are too far to the left, the clubface opens more at impact, creating a weaker shot.

Stance

An open or closed stance can dramatically affect the actual swing plane and cause a player to loop at the top of the backswing. Width of stance is also important. A player should be balanced and able to shift his or her weight easily. Too narrow a width and any shift of weight results in loss of balance. Too wide a width creates difficulties in shifting any weight at all.

Alignment

Aligning both the body and the clubface is essential before attempting a swing. Good swing movement is wasted if a

Precision striking Bernhard Langer demonstrates how to play a short-iron shot by striking down on the ball and then hitting the turf.

player doesn't aim in the right direction. This is the first checkpoint for any golfer who is having swing problems.

Posture

A player's posture can cause many problems with both strike and swing plane. A player who is too far bent over or very tall

WHAT IS A LOOP?

A loop is where the backswing is too flat or upright until the point at the top of the swing where it changes direction to a steeper or flatter angle. The clubhead does a "loop" in the air.

Width Creating width when swinging is essential to producing power. The extra space allows a player to produce a bigger arc—the club has farther to travel before it strikes the ball. This gives the player more time to accelerate. The player on the left illustrates poor width in the backswing whereas Jack Nicklaus (above) has the club higher above his head thus creating much more width.

may have issues with inconsistent striking, due to changes in posture during the swing.

Ball Position

The position of the ball is another huge factor in poor striking. Placing the ball too far forward causes thin (where the ball is struck too high on its surface and doesn't fly at the correct trajectory or distance), fat (where the club strikes the ground before the ball) or topped (where the ball is struck so high on its surface it doesn't leave the ground) shots. A ball that is too far back can produce the same effects, depending on how a player's swing alters to try to adapt.

Swing

Even a player who has a perfect setup needs to make the right movements throughout the swing. This is the reason the top pros produce similar and consistent results—they all swing differently, but their fundamentals are excellent.

Path of Club

The path of the club—called the swing path—relates to the hitting area, or zone. This is the two feet before impact, the area at impact and the two feet after impact. The path that the club travels through this area determines the direction the ball takes, so whatever happens during the swing outside this area has less relevance. However, the more movement in the body and swing-plane changes there are, the less likely you are to get the swing path correct.

The swing path indicates where the ball starts, and the position of the clubface in relation to the path determines where the ball finishes. The ideal swing path is inside–square–inside, and the path refers to the line of target. When starting the ball on the target line, the path just before impact should be on an inside arc of this line. At impact, the club should be square to the line, and after impact, the club follows again to the inside. This equates to a semicircle or half-moon shape.

SWING PATHS

An inside–to–outside path starts the ball off right, but depending on where the clubface is at impact, spin is produced, influencing the ball's flight once it has left the face. A closed clubface to the target line causes the ball to start right and finish left with a big hook. A square clubface to the target line creates a draw shot that starts to the right of the target and finishes on target. The worst scenario is an open clubface to the target. Here, the ball starts to the right of the target and finishes even farther right.

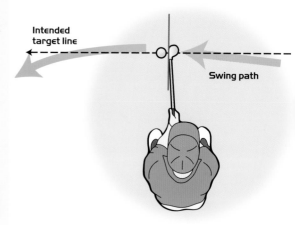

Intended target line

Swing path

At target A club traveling on an inside–square–inside path makes the ball start on the target line. This is the correct path through impact.

Right of target
A club traveling on an inside-to-outside path makes the ball start to the right of the target line.

Variations

Variations in swing path can make the ball off target at the start. An inside–to–outside swing path causes the ball to move to the right of the target. An outside–to–inside swing path starts the ball to the left of the target. This doesn't mean the ball finishes off target, because swing path has nothing to do with spin, but it determines where the ball starts its journey.

Swing path is extremely difficult to see, but double-checking alignment should be a priority. Tour professionals always put down a club when practicing to ensure that everything is correct. Once they are satisfied, observing where the ball starts while practicing indicates swing path. Looking at the divots after a shot and determining where they point gives an indication of the club's swing path.

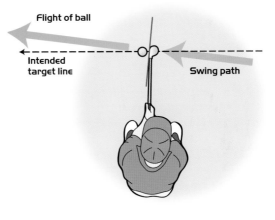

Flight of ball

Intended target line

Swing path

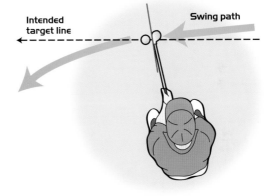

Intended target line

Swing path

Left of target A club traveling on an outside–to–inside path makes the ball start to the left of the target line.

7

Choosing the Right Clubs

The vast choice of styles, materials, shafts, weights and grips available has made it extremely difficult to decide which golf clubs to buy. This chapter is dedicated to helping with some of the choices that players are faced with, both on and off the course.

Club selection Millions of golfers, like other consumers, may be seduced by the slick advertising and endorsements for the latest hi-tech product, but often it may not be right for that golfer's ability or where they regularly play.

On the Course

On the course, it's time for golfers to relax and enjoy the scenery, unless, the scenery is a lake or a thicket of trees that is in the way. Course management is a way of knocking shots off your score— simply by playing smarter.

A golfer needs to be aware of shots that he or she can or cannot hit. Imagine a player standing on a tee with a bunker at 230 yards (210 m) in the center of the fairway and another 20 yards (18 m) is needed to clear the bunker. If this player carries the ball, on average, 220 yards (200 m), he or she must use a club that makes it impossible to reach the bunker. One of the keys to golf is knowing your limits and playing within them. Even pros are aware of their limits.

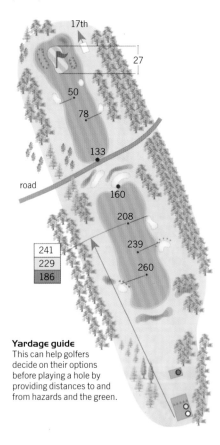

Yardage guide
This can help golfers decide on their options before playing a hole by providing distances to and from hazards and the green.

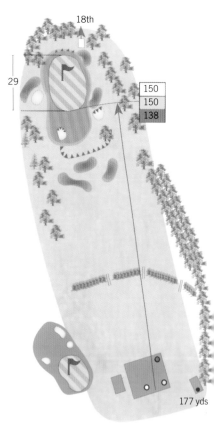

CONSIDER YOUR OPTIONS

When Tiger Woods won the 2006 Open Championship at Royal Liverpool Golf Club in England, the course measured 7,258 yards (6,637 m), and he struck his driver only once. Being an extremely long hitter, Woods could have tried to overpower the course, but he felt that the penalties were too harsh. Hitting either three woods or irons from the tee ensured that he stayed away from bunkers and any other potential dangers. He shot 18 under par and won by two shots.

Playability An iron with a large cavity is easier to use, but experienced players who like to shape the ball might prefer a smaller head made from mild steel.

You may see them hitting drives that clear bunkers or lakes at 300 yards (275 m), but they know they can hit these shots—and can probably hit 30 in a row the same way—so the risk is minimal.

The answer isn't always to play safe. For example: A golfer is playing a short par five of 470 yards (430 m), but the fairway is tight and lined with trees—is it worth risking a missed fairway for extra length? On weighing up the risk, the answer should be yes. There is a very good chance of reaching the green in two, but the penalty for missing the fairway is only trees, so if the drive lands there, the player accepts it, pitches out and can still make par. However, if the trees are out of bounds, the answer is no—the risk far outweighs

the reward. Knowing how far a player hits each club is a big factor in being successful at course management and staying out of trouble. Scoring well is much more difficult from rough, trees and water.

It's not only long shots that require attention, however. If a player has missed a green and has very little room between him or her and the flag, the best option may be to forget about the flag and simply get the ball onto the green. Showing off and attempting to get the ball close can result in many more dropped shots.

Risk vs. reward The 13th at Augusta National Golf Club in Georgia, the home of the U.S. Masters, is a short par five, but is riddled with dangers. Some players choose to go for the green—and glory—in two, but this brings the creek into play.

How to Play Different Types of Courses

There are thousands of golf courses around the world, and every one is different in terms of length and design. Before playing any course, the course style and weather conditions should be considered so that the golfer is prepared for what lies ahead.

The first of many factors to consider is whether the course is modern or established. If it is modern, the likelihood is that all the trees have not grown big enough to pose any problems and may still be protected to allow trees to mature. So, any player who hits a ball that finishes close to a young tree is likely to receive relief with no penalty. Modern courses also tend to be much more generous with fairway widths, so players must ensure they have a driver in their bags.

If the course is older and established, the fairways are likely to be narrow and tree lined, so a player should consider a fairway wood, long irons and a hybrid, as these clubs give more accuracy when used from the tee. As the ball wasn't driven as far when they were first designed, established courses also tend to be much shorter in length, so the emphasis here is on accuracy rather than distance.

Treelined The Old Course at Sunningdale Golf Club in England is heavily treelined, and accuracy is the main factor in good scoring. Sacrificing length for accuracy is recommended when playing here.

Course Style

The style of the course is another factor that all players, including top professionals, have to consider before playing. Before you play, you need to consider the following questions:

- Are the greens soft or hard?
- Are the fairways wide or narrow?
- Are the greens protected or raised?
- Is the course at a high altitude?

If the greens are protected by hazards, either sandtraps or water, or raised, the option of trying to run the ball onto the green is taken away from you. Many modern courses are raised or have lakes in front of greens to discourage this type of shot. In these instances, it is beneficial to choose clubs and a ball that create more height, enabling the player to land the ball on the green by achieving more carry.

Danger everywhere The par-three 17th at Sawgrass in Florida is an island green surrounded by water—the only option is to hit a good shot onto the green.

Escaping trouble Jose Maria Olazabal plays out of the trees, after an attempt to go for the green.

Using fairway woods instead of long irons or hybrids is an excellent choice because of the height they produce, as is using a higher-spinning ball for extra height.

Altitude

Altitude can affect the ball's carry up to 10 percent. Though this doesn't sound like a lot, it's the difference between hitting the ball 150 yards (137 m) and 165 yards (150 m). For most golfers, this equates to one extra club. Many touring professionals don't like playing at high altitudes because of the change in distances.

American Style vs. Links

Golf courses are constructed differently depending on the ground, grass and weather. The two main types of courses are known as American-style and links-style and are different in appearance, design and construction.

Change in elevation When striking a shot from above or below the target, adjustments in club selection must be made. This shot at Mont Tremblant Resort in Québec, Canada requires less club owing to the drop in elevation.

American-style courses tend to be found inland, have lush grass and are watered well, with lakes, large bunkers and big sloping greens. They are considered attractive golf courses because of the green grass and the blue water features. Most are heavily wooded, too.

A links-style course is very different. This type of course is located near the coast and is protected by the wind, so water hazards and trees are seldom used. The rough is usually long and thick, making it extremely punishing. The fairway grass tends to be much shorter, and players find it more difficult to create height and solid strikes. Golfers who play regularly on American-style courses are likely to choose irons that have a large sole, as they almost bounce off the lush grass. When playing on a links-style course, the grass is much shorter and tighter and the ground firmer, so this type of club is more difficult to use. In this case, a player needs to drive into the back of the ball, creating a crisp strike. Any iron with a larger sole is likely to bounce off the hard ground and cause inconsistent striking.

Rain

The weather forecast has a huge impact on the playing conditions of a course. If a course has been rained on for the past two days, it will be very soft, resulting in greens that hold a ball more easily. However, the fairways will actually play wider, as the ball won't run as far on wet ground.

Sole design An iron with a narrow sole is easier to strike from tight, short grass; while an iron with a larger, more rounded sole benefits from lush turf.

Links golf Carnoustie Golf Links in Scotland is renowned for being one of the most difficult courses in the world, partly due to the high winds and deep bunkers.

A player should bring along the necessary extras if it rains during play, including waterproof pants, a jacket and an extra pair of gloves. Gloves lose all grip when wet, so consider using all-weather synthetic gloves, as they are constructed to grip better in the rain. Extra towels are also essential. Most golf bags are built for lightness and are made from nylon, so the clubs' grips have very little protection against the rain and need drying before every shot. Finally, don't forget an umbrella.

Rain also results in a course that plays longer because of the loss of roll and wet, soft greens that are more likely to hold the ball. The use of a slightly harder ball is common as it helps gain more distance.

Warm climates When playing in warmer places, such as at the Chung Shan Hot Spring Golf Club in China, a player must remember that warm air makes a ball travel farther.

Heat vs. Cold

If the course has been baked in sunshine for weeks, it will play differently. The fairways are likely to be much harder, so the ball runs a long way, making the course effectively shorter. The greens are also likely to be dryer and harder, so many players use a softer golf ball to create more spin to help stop the ball more quickly. Many courses have sprinkler systems and water the greens (and sometimes the fairways) when the weather has been especially dry.

Temperatures also affect the ball's flight. As the weather gets warmer, a golf ball becomes easier to compress and travels slightly farther. Alternatively, when playing during the winter or under cold conditions, the ball tends to travel a shorter distance. In addition, humidity affects the ball's flight. Golfers who play in locations with high humidity find the ball travels slightly less than normal, due to the wetter, heavier air.

Rainy courses Synthetic gloves are essential for playing in the rain as they are customized to help retain a player's grip. Mark Hirzel also makes good use of an umbrella as he putts on the green during a rainstorm on Oahu, Hawaii.

Wind

If the forecast is for wind, a player should consider trying to fly the ball much lower, as strong wind makes scoring very difficult. Even if a player feels that he or she doesn't have the capability to hit lower shots, he or she can still choose equipment that will do it for them, such as long irons instead of fairway woods. It might also be beneficial to take one or two clubs more and hit shots more softly to reduce spin. Also, less loft keeps the ball down out of the wind.

Windy courses Johanna Westerberg of Sweden deals with windy conditions on the 6th fairway at Clearwater Golf Course in New Zealand. Players aim to lower their ball flight when playing in blustery conditions.

Picking Your 14 Clubs

According to the rules of golf, a player can carry up to a maximum of 14 clubs in his or her bag at any one time. However, there is no regulation covering which 14 clubs can be carried. With so much choice available, it has become extremely difficult to select the correct ones. The golf set composition should be the best clubs for that individual, matching the player's strengths and weaknesses.

A golf set composition usually consists of the following:

- One driver
- One three wood
- Either a five and seven wood or a two and three hybrid
- Medium irons (four, five and six)
- Short irons (seven, eight and nine)
- Wedges (any combination of pitching, gap, sand and lob wedge)
- One putter

This is only a suggestion, and a player is entitled to choose any combination that he or she likes.

Irons

Generally, it's best to eliminate all the long irons, the one and two irons and even the

Hazards Holes at the famed Augusta National Golf Club have become more difficult over the years, with well-placed hazards at times forcing the golfer to play safe, for example using shorter irons to avoid the water on this par 3.

three iron, because they are unforgiving and are the most difficult clubs to hit. Replacing these long irons with either two hybrids or two fairway woods is a much safer option. Almost all golfers carry four, five, six, seven, eight and nine irons (plus a putter) in their bags, and this already takes up half the set.

Wedges

Wedges are known as the scoring clubs, and are difficult to get right. Because the short game plays such a big role in

Doglegs With doglegs, a golfer has two clear choices: attempt to go for glory with a wood or long iron aiming blindly for the green, or play the "percentages," and take two shots.

Blind shots Some shots are blind and a player must aim at a spot other than the fairway. This is when a yardage guide becomes useful. A golfer may be tempted to play short to see the green, though this may land the golfer in the rough, which will require a smart choice of club, usually a shorter iron to cut through the thick grass.

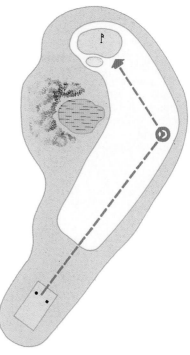

your scoring, the wedges need to be correct.

It is likely that if a player wants to keep a pitching, gap, sand and lob wedge, he or she must sacrifice a club elsewhere in the set—normally in the fairway-wood or long-iron area. It is possible to manage with three wedges, but because pitching and chipping can save so many shots, it is a decision only a player can make.

Longest Clubs

For the longest clubs, a driver is automatic, as is a three wood. This leaves the choice of either one or two clubs, depending on the wedge selection. Since the one, two and three irons have been left out due to their unforgiving natures, the options are either a two or three hybrid or a five wood. If there are two open club spaces, it is possible to choose a two and three hybrid or a five and seven wood.

Variations

Many players, certainly professionals, have a huge selection of clubs at their disposal, but many keep their irons for one season or more. With drivers

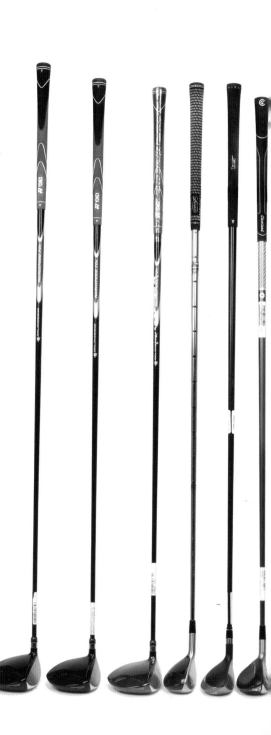

The correct 14 The perfect combination of clubs does not exist—only the right mix for each individual and the course being played.

and, more commonly, putters, however, pros sometimes change from week to week. A particular putter may be heavier and might work better on slightly slower greens, or perhaps a driver may fly the ball lower on a windy course. Given the variables, the choices are endless. Some players have been known to carry two putters.

When Phil Mickelson won the 2006 Masters he carried two drivers that were weighted differently—one for a draw shot and one for a fade.

With so many options and expectations, every player's bag is likely to have a different combination. The important thing to remember is that a player should focus on his or her strengths. If pitching and chipping is what a player does best, leaving out a wedge or two will give less options and most likely result in poorer shots overall. If a player's long game is weak, adding another long iron, hybrid or fairway wood isn't going to make him or her hit any better.

8

Purchasing Clubs

Once the trial of finding the right clubs and the fitting have been completed, the next and final step is deciding exactly which clubs to buy. With so many manufacturers to choose from and hundreds of potential models available, this is another difficult choice.

What to buy? The average golfer will be dazzled by the huge selection of shiny new clubs when they go to their retail outlet, but careful consideration of all the options is crucial. And spending thousands of dollars on a new set is not necessary or even wise for the average golfer, as design variations may not suit their game.

What to Consider

Different factors appeal to different players, leading them to buy certain models based on price, advice or advertising. The more information a player has about models of clubs—whether it be from a professional or an Internet blog—helps in making a purchase decision. The key is not to rush.

A player doesn't want to spend $1,000 on a set of clubs to find that he or she doesn't like playing with them only a month or two later. Gaining helpful purchase information takes time, but the end result is a happy golfer who is confident that all the equipment is custom fitted to his or her specifications. Because golf is based so much on confidence, players who have the smallest details incorrect know immediately that something is wrong, no matter how trivial. A misaligned grip can be enough

Buying brands Spending a lot of money on top quality, big-name brands doesn't always equate to the best equipment for an individual.

to change the feel of the entire club. Just because one club suits one person doesn't mean that it will suit another player.

The Pros

Top professionals have contracts to use certain equipment and are paid to play with their clubs. The equipment is adjusted to

Pro choice Top pros use the main manufacturers not only because of their contracts but also because of the high-quality equipment.

the pros' specific needs. But buying Cobra woods or Titleist irons just because a famous touring professional uses them is a waste of time. A driver will help even less, because amateurs generally can't hit the ball beyond 300 yards (275 m).

It's a different story with putters. A pro who uses a certain putter to win a major tournament creates demand for that club, as amateurs are just as likely to hole putts as professionals.

Professional Opinion

If your teeth hurt, you go to a dentist; if your car breaks down, you get it fixed by a mechanic; if your golf swing needs to be perfected or if you need custom fitting, you visit a professional. Though it seems obvious, this is a rule that should always be followed.

All of us know many golf "experts"— just walk into any clubhouse bar and

Professional advice Advice is free, and PGA professionals are always happy to answer questions.

there will be a line of people ready to tell you what is wrong with your game, what equipment you need to purchase or how to putt just like them (which is usually badly). This is the nature of the game, and most of the time the information your friends give, though well meaning, slows you down or even makes things worse.

It is easy to listen to other golfers, especially if they are better players, but they are not golf professionals, so you are probably wasting your time taking their advice blindly. Every PGA establishment has fully qualified PGA professionals who are trained to give advice on every golf-related subject, no matter how trivial. These professionals have the knowledge and training to help improve a player's game.

Budget

The cost of a full set of golf clubs, including woods, irons, wedges and a putter, can run into thousands of dollars. Though every player would love the opportunity to purchase the most expensive equipment, sometimes this isn't possible. It is very important to have a budget and set spending limits.

The golf market has a vast range of clubs for sale, with a driver costing anywhere from $30 to $500. Sets start at $100 and go to more than $1,000. The main reason golfers now spend so much on equipment is because it is updated so quickly. New models and designs are launched annually, and sometimes players simply want to have the best and latest products.

Top manufacturers spend millions on research and development, marketing and design to make sure their products get noticed and test well. The components used are top-spec steel and graphite. The grips and shafts are branded.

The budget option is usually a product from a smaller company that makes reproductions of clubs already on the market. They all have a grip, shaft and a head, but the components are inferior, with less testing and very little advertising.

Used Clubs

Another option for golfers on a restricted budget is to purchase used clubs. Used golf equipment is a very good decision financially, as models change so frequently. This makes any previous models obsolete and worth very little—the same principle utilized in the used-car trade. Clubs that are less than one year old can be bought for less than one half

IRONS

One option for some golfers is to put aside more money for a set of irons. Golfers tend to keep irons much longer than drivers or putters, and though the initial cost can be expensive, modern irons are very durable and are likely to last for many years if they are well maintained.

the original price. Retail outlets have a used section where players can trade in their old sets or upgrade to new ones. Websites such as eBay are also good sources of used clubs. If players do their homework and know what to look out for, purchasing can be done on a tight budget.

Even if a player has previously had a club fitting and knows his or her specifications, buying secondhand can still be a good option. For example, if a player needs clubs that are half an inch longer and one degree upright, browsing through websites can uncover available clubs that have that spec. Alternatively, a player may have a particular model in mind and can find only a standard set. If this is the case, the player can take the clubs to a local professional, along with the required specs, and the alterations can be made at a reasonable cost. The main disadvantage in buying secondhand is that a player has fewer options on the grip, shaft, and so on. Though these alterations can be done after the purchase, they are time consuming. In the end, the more alterations needed, the more the cost increases. There is also the comfort of knowing that when you buy new equipment from an established retailer or PGA professional, the goods are legitimate. A risk of purchasing used clubs, especially online, is that there is always the chance of being conned into buying replicas or fake clubs.

Secondhand Balls

It isn't just golf clubs that are available to buy secondhand. Many players purchase used golf balls that have been pulled from a lake, cleaned and resold. Though these used balls look like new, it doesn't mean they'll fly like a new ball. A ball's stability and potential flight distance are determined by its dimples. Every time a ball is struck, the dimples get worn; the same thing happens every time a ball is washed or cleaned. The more the dimples get worn, the more the ball flies like it has no dimples at all. The effect is a huge loss in distance. Tests have proven that a golf ball struck with a driver by a good player can travel 280 yards (255 m). The same player using the same club at the same speed hitting a ball without dimples loses more than one half of the distance. Cuts and scuffs can also affect a ball's flight. When it comes to golf balls, spend a little extra and always buy new.

Used equipment Buying used clubs is a cost-effective way of purchasing as long as you know the specifications required. Be sure to double-check serial numbers with manufacturers to ensure that the products are legitimate.

Manufacturer Preference

With so much choice in equipment it can be difficult to decide how much to spend, where to make the purchase and whether custom fitting is necessary. It is also important to keep in mind the differences between manufacturers, to know what they offer and why a player might choose one over another.

Currently the biggest names in golf equipment manufacturing are:

- Callaway
- Cobra
- FootJoy
- Mizuno
- Ping
- TaylorMade
- Titleist

Secondary manufacturers include:

- Adidas
- Cleveland
- Nike
- Wilson

These are all well-known, advertised brands and are used by the majority of tour pros. But there are also hundreds of smaller companies on the golf market.

Brand Loyalty

There are many different reasons golfers choose certain manufacturers over others. Some are recommended a brand by friends or family members. Other golfers just go by appearance, and some want to match all their equipment. For example, if a player has a Mizuno bag and irons, he

Manufacturers Until recently, most players chose to buy equipment from manufacturers like Titleist, TaylorMade and Ping, which sell only golf-related products. Now other sports companies, such as Adidas and Nike, are major players in the golf market.

or she might want to have everything branded Mizuno. This is known as being brand loyal and is one of the reasons companies produce such a vast range of accessories. Umbrellas, flight bags, towels, gloves, shoes, golf balls and even tees are add-ons that are produced for brand-loyal golfers.

Golfers may also stick with a manufacturer based on previous success. For example, if a Cleveland lob wedge previously worked well but now needs to be replaced, buying another Cleveland lob wedge probably makes the most sense.

Advertising

The differences between the golf equipment produced at the higher end of the market are so small that there is little to separate them, which is why millions is spent on advertising.

Branding All three woods do the same job, but differ in appearance and price. Confidence in a brand name can be the deciding purchasing factor.

Accessories Most manufacturers produce a range of accessories alongside their clubs—including umbrellas, gloves, caps, belts, towels, bags and more—for brand-loyal golfers.

A company can produce a set of irons with a superb feel that tests much better than any other iron set, but without effective promotion no sales will be made.

Like all consumers, golfers can be persuaded by the power of advertising. Companies spend millions of dollars on marketing and advertising because brand awareness is so crucial. Certain brand names are known worldwide, and this is due to the advertising behind them—the red-and-white Coca-Cola logo, the Nike "swoosh" and the red arches of McDonald's are instantly recognizable around the world, which makes people choose them over their rivals.

Celebrity Endorsement

Golf companies always want to sign the best players. When a player is doing well in a big tournament and uses a Ping bag and a putter with the logos in full view, this equates to an incredible amount of valuable airtime—airtime that, if purchased, would cost millions.

The same is true in television and print advertising. If a golf company hires a celebrity to promote their products, viewers and readers are much more likely to remember the brand or product. This could spell the difference between a player buying a Nike or TaylorMade driver. The days of golf being seen as a game for old, wealthy men has now been replaced by the perception of a cool sport that people of all ages and backgrounds want to play. Producing ads that feature movie stars or famous musicians enhances the credibility of that brand. If Tiger Woods plays with a Nike driver, for instance, many golfers feel that Nike must produce great equipment.

Endorsement As the highest-ranked golfer in his home country of France, and a rising talent on the European tour, Grégory Havret will attract the major golf manufacturers, who will be certain of exposure in markets where golf is not one of the top sports.

Some golfers ignore all the advertising and any words of wisdom that their family or friends offer and base their purchasing decisions on appearance and instinct. Sometimes a club just feels right, and regardless of the manufacturer or cost, the club gets purchased—sometimes at great expense. However, most golfers are less impulsive and try out the equipment first, basing their decisions on what performs best for them and what is right for their game. This is the correct way to determine brand choice.

9

Ladies' Clubs

Ladies' clubs are similar to men's
clubs in that they share the same basic
components, but they differ in other ways,
such as weight, length and feel. This chapter
explores the changes in ladies' clubs,
and how these improve the game.

Michelle Wie The phenomenal success and high profile of Wie has
attracted many girls to the game around the world and led her to be
included in *Time* magazine's list of "100 People Who Shape Our World."
She intends to be the first woman to play in the Masters.

Club Cosmetics

Years ago, female golfers used men's clubs that had been cut down slightly. This made the clubs a little more playable, but they were still extremely heavy. Today, ladies' golf is a rapidly growing sector of the game and there are almost as many different types of clubs, shafts, grips and balls available for women as there are for men.

Ladies' clubs are easy to spot when on display—they are usually colored so they stand out. Grips and shafts might be pink, red, purple or orange. Even the clubhead is likely to contain some color enhancement. Bright colors are also used for accessories, from bags and gloves to shoes and towels. Manufacturers realize that ladies' golf is booming, and companies spend money on ladies' versions of the latest products because of this high demand.

More women play golf today than ever before, and ladies' golf has become more popular with spectators of both sexes for a very simple reason: ladies' tournaments are more fun to watch, on television or live.

There are inherent physical differences between male and female players. While many female players are athletic and strong, men usually have the advantage when it comes to power and distance. Men often use their strength to overpower

Karrie Webb Webb was the first player to surpass $1 million in single-season earnings on the LPGA tour, and is one of the most successful in women's golf, with seven majors.

courses, whereas women are more strategic and are known for their controlled shots. Though ladies' equipment is built to the same high standards as men's, there are still many differences between them.

Miscela range These clubs are produced by TaylorMade—one of the few manufacturers to offer a complete matching set for women, from woods to wedges.

LADIES' CLUBS

Ladies' clubs are usually finished with pastel colors. The design and technology is the same as men's clubs, but the swing weight is lower. This is achieved through a lighter shaft and less weight in the head, enabling players to generate good clubhead speed and distance.

iron

TF Gamer iron
Similar in design to the men's version, this iron has reduced weight in the head and shaft for extra playability.

hybrid

driver

Ping Rhapsody hybrid
This club has higher loft options than the men's version. It also has a shorter shaft for more control.

TaylorMade Burner driver This club has the same shape as the men's version but higher loft options, a lighter shaft and head, and a thinner grip.

wood

Mizuno MX-700 three wood Similar to the men's version but with a shorter, lighter shaft and a thinner grip; this wood generates control and distance.

Swing Speed

To achieve high clubhead speed, a combination of hand speed, body drive and rotation is necessary. The average swing speed of a woman is 60 mph (95 kph), which produces a ball speed of approximately 84 mph (135 kph).

On average, women are smaller than men and have less strength, and most ladies' clubs are constructed with these principles in mind. The flex of a woman's shaft is much softer than a man's owing to the reduction in speed. The shaft doesn't bend as much and is more likely to return the face square at impact—the shaft flex matches the swing speed. Stronger female players who swing the club more aggressively consequently have a faster swing speed, and they require a shaft to match. So a woman who

Acceleration Natalie Gulbis plays a pitch with a shortened backswing. She looks to accelerate into the ball to impart maximum spin.

Clubhead speed Michelle Wie demonstrates the need for acceleration as her club drives through the turf.

swings at 70 mph (112 kph) requires a seniors' flex shaft; a swing speed of 80 mph (128 kph) requires a men's flex.

Because not everyone buys clubs that are custom fit, manufacturers have to produce stock items. All ladies' shafts reading "flex 1" are intended for a swing speed of 60 mph (95 kph). Many top female pros use either men's senior flex or men's regular flex because of the extra power they produce, but consideration is

Overswing An overswing is the wrong way to create distance and is a common mistake for female golfers. The arms tend to bend at the top of the swing owing to the lack of wrist strength.

Posture Another common fault is the failure to maintain posture throughout a swing making it difficult to strike the ball consistently.

made for female golfers when they play courses. Rather than playing from the men's tee, which can make the course very long for many, women often play from a ladies' tee, which can be anything from 10 to 70 yards (9–65 m) closer to the green. This enables golf courses to be accessible to all standards of players.

Swing speed is measured in the same way for women as it is for men. A launch monitor or swing-speed machine registers an average speed, and from this speed, a shaft flex is determined.

Though shafts for women are generally more flexible, they are usually thinner, allowing for thinner grips as women tend to have smaller hands than men.

Loft

Women who produce a swing speed of 60 mph (95 kph) often have a problem achieving height, even more so with a driver. Because of the lack of power, the ball is not launched especially high and has less spin, so distance is lacking. The average loft on a ladies' club is 12° or 13°, and in some cases, a three wood is the better option. By adding loft, both height and spin are increased, which leads to greater distance.

Height

Height differences between men and women lead to large variations in swing. The reduced height in a woman is more likely to result in a flatter posture. This posture causes one major problem: the player tends to stand too tall, creating a flat swing plane.

A flat swing plane results in an angle of attack that is too shallow, leading to a too-clean strike. A reduction in height and spin, combined with a slower swing speed, can cause problems for many female players; the loss in distance is staggering.

Then and Now

If a comparison is made between female golfers 10–20 years ago and female players today, the physical changes are very noticeable.

Benefits of height A taller player can create a bigger arc, which increases distance, whereas a shorter player has a more compact swing.

Modern female golfers are taller, which aids their posture. They are also more athletic, which helps them rotate better. In addition, the athleticism produces smaller busts, allowing women to swing their arms around their chests without anything getting in the way.

Swing Arc

On average, men are three or four inches (8–10 cm) taller than women and have a wider swing arc. A bigger or wider arc pushes a club farther away from the ball during the swing, so it becomes easier to generate more power. This is a plus for distance; however, with more distance comes less control. So, ultimately, women are known for their controlled shots and men for power and distance.

Modern female golfers In the past 10 years, professional female golfers have changed in appearance and are more athletic, with smaller chests and stronger arms and wrists.

BUST AND OVERSWING

The bust is another factor in the swing of women. It can cause a flat takeaway or backswing, which needs to be altered by the player during the swing (known as a loop), but unless done perfectly it creates a downswing that is much too steep. This action creates a lot of wrist action and very little turn, usually resulting in an overswing. The overswing is an attempt to create more clubhead speed. This can work with men or women who have strong wrists, but generally an overswing produces a deceleration into the ball. Many women benefit more from a shorter backswing and acceleration through impact, using their wrists.

Custom fit The measurement from a player's fingertips to the floor is a big factor in determining club length.

Weight

Rhythm Using rhythm and timing, Paula Creamer allows the weight of her club to do most of the work in propelling the ball.

Women generate less power than men, so their equipment has slight alterations to help produce strength elsewhere.

Shafts

In a driver, a men's graphite shaft weighs 2.1–2.3 oz. (60–65 grams), while a ladies' shaft is only 1.6–1.75 oz. (45–50 grams) in weight. This reduction in weight makes the club easier to move faster; extra clubhead speed is created without losing control.

Men usually have steel shafts for stability and weight, but women normally use graphite shafts owing to their lighter weight and ease of use.

Swing Weight

Swing weight and actual weight are other areas where ladies' clubs are significantly different than men's. A reduced swing weight removes the feeling of weight in the head, giving a female player more chance to achieve power. As both the shaft and head are lighter, the club weighs less, too, again improving the speed of the swing.

The weight of the club is of huge importance not only because of the power that it helps generate but also because of its feel. A club with a swing weight that is too high feels too heavy in the head, and a player has very little control over it. A club with a swing weight that is too low can have the same effect—a lack of control. It is important to find the right weight for each player; men's and ladies' averages are simply stock

SWING WEIGHT COMPARISON

Iron	4	5	6	7	8	9	PW	AW	SW
TaylorMade Burner Plus for MEN									
Club Length	39"	38.5"	38"	37.5"	37"	36.5"	36.25"	36.25"	36"
Swing Weight	D2.5	D2.5	D2.5	D2.5	D2.5	D2.5	D3.5	D3.5	D5
TaylorMade Burner Plus for WOMEN									
Club Length	38"	37.5"	37"	36.5"	36"	35.5"	35.75"	35.75"	35"
Swing Weight	C6.5	C6.5	C6.5	C6.5	C6.5	C6.5	C7.5	C7.5	C9

standards that manufacturers produce and are not always correct for everyone. When purchasing a set of irons, it is imperative that the swing weights match. A set with contrasting swing weights is likely to result in a player never getting used to the feel. Irons are measured by a standard swing-weight scale, with men's often D0

Benefit of weight Extra weight in a club can sometimes be useful, as demonstrated by Lorena Ochoa. She uses the extra weight in her sand wedge to slide through the sand in this trap.

Length and swing weight Ladies' clubs are slightly shorter and lighter than men's.

or D1 and ladies' between C5 and C7. Swing weight in other clubs, such as drivers and wedges, varies, but they have different uses. A driver is designed for power and distance and should be fitted in a way that creates the most amount of each. Wedges are used around the greens, from bunkers or on the rough, and their extra weight is essential for these types of shots.

Length

The length of a club is related to the height of the player. The length of a standard ladies' club is between one half and one inch (1.5–3 cm) shorter than a men's club, reflecting the average height ratio between men and women. The length can be altered if required.

Shorter clubs are easier to control, and allow the female golfer to feel more comfortable at address and maintain control over the shot itself. The reduction in weight from a shorter club can also assist with generating more clubhead speed.

Taller players Laura Davies, at five feet 10 inches (175 cm), uses her height to gain distance.

Drivers

Some female pros like to use drivers with a men's-length shaft. The extra length helps create a bigger arc and more power. Sometimes straighter hitters are happy to trade accuracy for extra yardage. Alternatively, on the men's tour, pros are known to shorten their drivers for the opposite effect.

Power Carly Booth drives all her body weight into the ball for extra distance.

Follow-through The result of a clubhead accelerating through impact is a long follow-through, as shown by Julieta Granada.

Players who can generate a great amount of clubhead speed and power tend to be less accurate than shorter hitters, so some reduce the length of their drivers by one inch or more to give extra control. Many have found no loss in distance, and because of the extra control, they find they can strike the ball from the middle more often.

Hand Size/Grip

Compared to men, women tend to have smaller hands and shorter fingers. To accommodate this, ladies shafts' are usually smaller in diameter so that slightly thinner grips can be used. A thinner grip gives a woman a firmer hold on a club, which in turn provides more control.

A good grip is very important, but if the grip size in incorrect, it is almost impossible to hold a club properly. Grips that are too thick result in an ineffective, often-changing hand grip. More pressure is created because of the lack of a solid hold. Grips that are too thin can have a similar effect; a player almost smothers the grip and has to hold on tightly.

Gloves
Though not every player wears them, gloves are a useful addition. They give extra grip when the hands get sweaty or wet. A glove should fit snugly; if a glove is too big, it moves and

Grip Women with smaller hands may opt for the baseball grip, where all the fingers hold onto the club for added control.

creates friction, leading to blisters and a lack of club control.

Gloves come in two styles: leather and synthetic. A good-quality leather glove is very thin and soft and gives premium feel, but often at a premium price. Being thinner doesn't result in durability; a leather glove lasts for perhaps four or five rounds at most. Synthetic gloves are much tougher, cost less, can last many rounds and provide extra grip during wet weather. Leather gloves tend to lose grip as they get wet.

Top pros always play with the best quality leather gloves and often use two or three in one round. This is great if they are given to the golfers for free, but, for most, a mix of leather gloves for dry weather and synthetic for wetter days is a good choice.

Glove preference
Annika Sörenstam keeps her glove on when executing a pitch; other players prefer to remove it for all short shots.

Pairs of gloves
Though usually worn only on the left hand, some women like to wear gloves on both hands for extra grip.

PUTTING

Many professionals and amateurs choose to remove their gloves for shorter shots, as they believe the gloves can remove the feel aspect. This is a reasonable point, and almost all pros remove their gloves when putting.

Feel Like many other professionals, Michelle Wie chooses to remove her glove while putting. This gives her slightly more feel for the pace of the ball.

Further Resources

Associations

North America
CPGA (Canadian Professional Golfers' Association)
    13450 Dublin Line, RR#1
    Acton, Ontario L7J 2W7
    Phone: (800) 782-5764
    Fax: (519) 853-5449
    www.cpga.com
PGA (Professional Golfers' Association of America)
    100 Avenue of the Champions
    Palm Beach Gardens, FL 33418
    Phone: (561) 624-8400
    www.pga.com
USGA (United States Golf Association)
    P.O. Box 708
    Far Hills, NJ 07931
    Phone: (908) 234-2300
    E-mail: testcenter@usga.org
    www.usga.org

Europe
EGU (English Golf Union)
    The National Golf Centre, Woodhall Spa
    Lincolnshire LN10 6PU, U.K.
    Tel: (44) (0)1526 354500
    Fax: (44) (0)1526 354020
    E-mail: info@englishgolfunion.org
    www.englishgolfunion.org
R&A (The Royal and Ancient Golf Club of St. Andrews)
    St. Andrews, Fife KY16 9JD, U.K.
    Phone: (44) (0)1334 460000
    Fax: (44) (0)1334 460001
    www.randa.org

Australasia
PGAAU (Professional Golfers' Association of Australia)
    Sandhurst Club, 600 Thompson Road
    Sandhurst, Victoria 3977 Australia
    Phone: (61) (0)3 8320 1911
    Fax: (61) (0)3 9783 0000
    E-mail: info@pga.org.au
    www.pga.org.au

Manufacturers

Cobra www.cobragolf.com
Footjoy www.footjoy.com
Pinnacle www.pinnaclegolf.com
Titleist www.titleist.com
North America
    United States: Acushnet Company
    333 Bridge Street, Fairhaven
    MA 02719
    Phone: (800) 225-8500
    Canada: Acushnet Canada, Inc.
    500 Harry Walker Parkway North
    Newmarket, Ontario L3Y 8T6
    Phone: (905) 898-7575
Europe
    Acushnet Europe Ltd.
    Caxton Road, St. Ives, Huntingdon
    Cambridgeshire PE27 3LU, U.K.
    Phone: (44) (0)1480 301 114
Southeast Asia
    Acushnet Singapore Pte. Ltd.
    4 Changi South Lane, #03-01
    Nan Wah Building, Singapore 486127
    Phone: (65) 6788 9560
    E-mail: salessg@acushnetgolf.com

Australasia
Australia: Acushnet Australia Pty. Ltd.,
P.O. Box 112, Braeside, Victoria 3195
Phone: (61) (0)3 9540 5000
E-mail: salesau@acushnetgolf.com
New Zealand: Acushnet New Zealand Ltd
P.O. Box 5206, Mount Maunganui
Phone: (64) (07) 928 4880
E-mail: salesnz@acushnetgolf.com

Callaway www.callawaygolf.com
Ben Hogan www.benhogan.com
Odyssey www.odysseygolf.com
Top-Flite www.topflite.com
North America
United States: Callaway Golf Company
2180 Rutherford Road
Carlsbad, CA 92008-7328
Phone: (800) 588-9836
Canada: Callaway Golf Canada
250 Courtland Avenue
Concord, Ontario L4K 4N3
Phone: (800) 387-7000
E-mail: cacs@callawaygolf.com
Europe
Callaway Golf Europe
Unit A27, Barwell Business Park
Leatherhead Road, Chessington
Surrey KT9 2NY, U.K.
Phone: (44) (0)20 8391 0111
E-mail: europecustomerservice@
callawaygolf.com
Southeast Asia/Australasia
Callaway Golf South Pacific
16 Corporate Avenue
Rowville, Victoria 3178, Australia
Phone: (61) (0)3 9212 9400
E-mail: southpacificcs@callawaygolf.com

Cleveland www.clevelandgolf.com
North America
Cleveland Golf, 5601 Skylab Road
Huntington Beach, CA 92647
Phone: (800) 999-6262

Mizuno www.mizuno.com
North America
United States: Mizuno USA, Inc.
4925 Avalon Ridge Parkway
One Jack Curran Way
Norcross, GA 30071
Phone: (800) 966-1211
Canada: Mizuno Canada Ltd.
5206 Timberlea Boulevard
Mississauga, Ontario L4W 2S5
Phone: (800) 263-6256,
(905) 629-0500
Europe
Mizuno Corporation (U.K.)
Mizuno House, 612 Reading Road
Winnersh, Wokingham,
Berkshire RG41 5HE, U.K.
Phone: (44) (0)118 936 2100
Australasia
Mizuno Corporation Australia Pty. Ltd.
Unit 8, 677 Springvale Road
Mulgrave, Victoria 3170, Australia
Phone: (61) (0)3 9239 7100

Nike www.nike.com/nikegolf
North America
United States: Nike, Inc.
P.O. Box 4027, Beaverton
OR 97076-4027
Phone: (800) 344-6453
Canada: Nike Canada
175 Commerce Valley Drive
West Thornhill, Ontario L3T 7P6
Phone: (800) 663-6453
(416) 694-6453
E-mail: nike.canada@nike.com
Europe
Nike U.K.
1 Victory Way
Duxford International Business Park
Sunderland SR3 3XF, U.K.
Phone: (44) (0)191 401 6453
E-mail: consumer.affairs.gbr@nike.com

Southeast Asia
Nike Southeast Asia
300 Tampines Avenue 5, #04-02
Tampines Junction
Singapore 529653
Phone: (65) 6788 0990
Australasia
Australia: Nike Australia
28 Victoria Crescent
Abbotsford, Victoria 3067
Phone: (61) (0)3 9292 9335
New Zealand: Nike New Zealand
Level 1, The Mercari Centre
15 Mercari Way, Albany
Auckland 1330
Phone: (64) 9 414 2240

Ping www.pinggolf.com
North America
P.O. Box 82000
Phoenix, AZ 85071-2000
Phone (U.S.): (800) 4-PING-FIT
(474-6434)
Phone (Canada): (800) 352-7464

TaylorMade www.taylormadegolf.com
Adidas www.adidasgolf.com
North America
TaylorMade-adidas Golf NA HQ
5545 Fermi Court
Carlsbad, CA 92008-7324
Phone (U.S.): (866) 530-TMAG (8624)
Phone (Canada): (800) 668-9883
Europe
TaylorMade Court
Viables Business Park, Jays Close
Basingstoke, Hampshire RG22 4BS,
U.K.
Phone: (44) (0)800 8624 4653
Australasia
Australia HQ TaylorMade-adidas Golf
767 Springvale Road, Mulgrave,
Victoria 3170, Australia
Phone: (61) (0)3 9263 5299

Wilson www.wilson.com
North America
United States: Wilson Sporting Goods Co.
8750 W. Bryn Mawr Avenue
Chicago, IL 60631
Phone: (773) 714-6400
E-mail: askwilson@wilson.com
Canada: Amer Sports—Canada
2700 14th Avenue, Unit #1-4
Markham, Ontario L3R 0J1
Phone: (905) 470-9966
E-mail: info.canada@amersports.com
Europe
Amer Sports U.K. Ltd., Lyon Way
Frimley, Surrey GU16 7ER, U.K.
Phone: (44) (0)1276 404 800
E-mail: customer.service.internet@
amersports.com
Australasia
Amer Sports Australia Pty. Ltd.
18–20 Lakewood Boulevard
Braeside, Victoria 3195, Australia
Phone: (61) (0)3 8586 6666
E-mail: info@wilsonsports.com.au

Retail Outlets

www.edwinwattsgolf.com: U.S. retail store
specializing in both new and used golf
clubs
www.golfsmith.com: U.S. retail outlet that
also provides advice and a logo service
www.golfworks.com.au: Australian retailer
selling everything golf related, from
equipment to insurance and vacations
www.rockbottomgolf.com: International
website selling all major golf brands at
discounted prices
www.thesportshq.com: Europe-based
discount sports and golf retailer
www.tourspecgolf.com: Premium golf
clubs made for the Japanese market
but available worldwide

Books

Ben Hogan's Five Lessons: The Modern Fundamentals of Golf by Ben Hogan (Pocket, 1990)

Dave Pelz's Short Game Bible by Dave Pelz (Broadway Books, 1999)

Golfer's Logbook by Lee Pearce (Collins, 2008)

Golf for Dummies by Gary McCord (For Dummies, 2009)

The Golf Instruction Manual by Steve Newell (DK Adult, 2001)

Golf Is Not a Game of Perfect by Dr. Bob Rotella & Bob Cullen (Simon & Schuster, 1995)

Magazines

Asian Golf Monthly (Southeast Asia)
Phone: (65) 6323 2800
Fax: (65) 6323 2838
www.asiangolfmonthly.com

Australian Golf Digest
Phone (national): 1300 656 933
Fax: (61) (0)2 9279 3161
www.australiangolfdigest.com.au

Golf Australia
Phone (Sydney): 9901 6111
Phone (national free call): 1800 227 236
Phone (overseas): (61) (0)2 9901 6111
Fax: (61) (0)2 9901 6110
www.golfaustralia.com.au

Golf Digest (United States/Canada)
Phone: (800) 678-3927
www.golfdigest.com

Today's Golfer (Europe)
Phone: (44) (0)1733 468 243
Fax: (44) (0)1733 468 671
www.todaysgolfer.co.uk

Websites

www.asiantour.com: The Asian Tour is the official regional sanctioning body for professional golf in Asia, and this site lists all schedules and results

www.ausgolf.com.au: Provides information on courses, travel, equipment and golf headlines for Australia

www.europeantour.com: Features player profiles, plus schedules, results and order of merit for the European PGA tour

www.golfasian.com: Gives information about golf vacations and packages in Thailand

www.golfaustralia.org.au: Check here for news, statistics, retail information and Australian results

www.pgatour.com: PGA tour events, including scoring and player profiles, are featured on this comprehensive site

www.pgatour.com.au: Provides news, results and schedules for the Australian PGA tour

www.worldgolf.com: Includes reviews of clubs and worldwide golf destinations, plus all the latest game tips

Glossary

Address: A golfer's position when preparing to hit a ball.

Backspin: The spin on the ball applied by loft on the clubface. A skilled player may apply extra backspin to stop the ball rolling forward on landing.

Backswing: The first part of a swing, when the club is moved away from the ball to behind the shoulder.

Balata: A rubber cover used on a golf ball to help increase the spin rate.

Bladed club: An iron design that lacks a cavity in the back of the head.

Cavity-back club: A club design with more weight distributed on the perimeter of the back of the head, thus creating a cavity.

Chip: A short running shot with a medium iron from just off the edge of the green.

Composite driver: A club composed of two materials. Titanium and graphite are the most common elements.

Course management: The act of a player plotting his or her way around each hole and calculating every shot.

Custom fitting: The process of altering golf clubs to fit a player's individual requirements.

Divot: The sliver of turf cut after playing a shot.

Dogleg: A golf hole that turns at a sharp angle.

Downswing: The portion of a golf swing from the top of the backswing to the striking of the ball.

Draw: A shot with a slight controlled curve through the air, from right to left (for right-handed players).

Face: The surface of a clubhead that strikes the ball.

Face insert: The extra hard impact area set into the face of a wood.

Fade: A shot designed to curve slightly in the air, from left to right (for right-handed players).

Fairway woods: Two, three, four, five (and sometimes higher-numbered) woods, which are designed to be used when the ball is in play after a tee shot.

Flange: The broad sole of an iron club, particularly exaggerated on a sand wedge.

Flex: The bend of a club's shaft.

Force line: The line that indicates the initial direction of a golf ball.

Forged head: A clubhead that is constructed from mild steel.

Handicap: The rating of a player's skill relative to par for the course. For example, a 20-handicap player should complete a par-70 course with a score of 90. This stroke allowance permits players of unequal skills to compete on the same terms.

Hazard: Any permanent obstacle on a course such as a bunker or a ditch.

Hook: A faulty stroke when the ball curves to the left (for right-handed players).

Hosel: The extension to the clubhead into which the shaft fits.

Hybrid: A mixture of an iron and a wood club.

Launch: The direction the ball starts its journey as it leaves the clubface.

Launch angle: The angle in degrees that a ball leaves the clubface.

Launch monitor: A machine that registers the angle at which a ball comes off the clubface.

Lie: The position in which a ball comes to rest. Also, the angle between the clubhead and the shaft, which may vary to suit players of different heights.

Links-style course: A seaside golf course, typified by sand, turf and coarse grass, of the type where golf was first played.

Lob: A high-lofted shot that lands very softly.

Loft: The angle on the clubhead that produces more or less height; loft also makes the ball rise.

Long game: Distance shots, using woods, hybrids and long irons.

Long iron: Two, three or four iron clubs.

Medium iron: Five, six or seven iron clubs.

Muscle-back club: An iron design similar to a blade but with slightly altered weight on the back of the club.

Overswing: A swing that occurs when a player moves the club shaft past parallel to the ground on the backswing.

Perimeter-weighted club: A club with more weight placed around the outside area of the back of the head.

PGA: The Professional Golfers' Association, one of the governing bodies for golf in the world. Founded in 1916, it is the largest sporting organization in the world. The women's equivalent is the Ladies Professional Golf Association (LPGA).

Pitch: A short shot to the green, hit high so that the ball does not roll on landing.

Rough: The part of a golf course where the grass is grown the longest to punish wayward shots.

Running shot: A low-flighted shot that runs more than usual along the ground.

Scratch golfer: A player who is expected to play the course in par.

Short game: Any shot around the green that usually requires a short swing.

Short iron: The shortest iron in length—eight and nine irons and wedges.

Sidespin: The direction of spin on a ball.

Slice: A faulty shot that curves from left to right in the air (for right-handed players).

Sole: The underside of a clubhead.

Spine angle: The angle between a player's legs and back.

Sweet spot: The area on a clubface that gives the most power.

Swing arc: The line on which a club is swung.

Swing path: The line on which a club travels before impact.

Swing plane: The angle on which a club is swung.

Swing studio: An indoor room where swings can be analyzed.

Swing weight: The measure of balance and overall weight of a club. In a match set, all clubs should feel the same when swung.

Target line: The line going from a ball to the target.

Tee: The spot from which players hit their first shot on every hole.

Toe: The area of a clubhead farthest from the shaft.

Topspin: The direction of spin on a ball.

Torque: The twist in a shaft.

Wedge: A selection of the shortest and most-lofted irons; they can be anywhere from 46–64°.

Weighting: The weight placed in certain areas of a club.

Index

Acknowledgments

The publishers would like to thank the following companies for their invaluable assistance with the creation of this book: Callaway, Mizuno, Ping and TaylorMade.

Images: 1 Ping; 3 Mizuno; 6b Ping; 7t Getty Images/Scott Halleran; 7b Mizuno; 8t ©Phil Sheldon; 8b St Andrews University Photographic Collection; 9t&bl ©Phil Sheldon; 9br Ping; 10 © H Routledge/Phil Sheldon; 12 Corbis/Jerry Cooke; 13t Getty Images/ Maria Kostina; 13b ©P Inglis/Phil Sheldon; 14 & 15t ©Phil Sheldon; 15b Callaway Golf; 16t Ping; 17l Mizuno; 17r Ping; 18–19c © sebastiankiek/Fotolio.com; 20 TaylorMade; 21 & 22 ©Phil Sheldon; 23t Corbis/ Reuters/Paul Hanna; 23b Corbis/Viviane Moos; 24t Getty Images/Allsport/ J.D. Cuban; 24b, 25 & 26 Ping; 29 Mizuno; 32, 33b & 34r ©Phil Sheldon; 35 TaylorMade; 36 Ping; 37 TaylorMade; 38t & bl TaylorMade; 38br Ping; 39t & br Callaway Golf; 39bl Mizuno; 41 Corbis/Reuters/Marcelo del Pozo; 44 Ping; 45 & 46t TaylorMade; 46bl & br Mizuno; 47t Callaway Golf; 47bl TaylorMade; 47br Ping; 48t Mizuno; 49l & 50t Ping; 51 & 52l TaylorMade; 52t & br Mizuno; 52cr Ben Hogan/Callaway Golf; 52bl Ping; 54t & cl Mizuno; 54bl & br Ping; 55tl, bl, cr & br TaylorMade; 55tr Ping; 56br Mizuno; 58t Callaway Golf; 58b Ben Hogan/Callaway Golf; 59tl Ping; 59tr Callaway Golf; 59cl & bl Mizuno; 59br TaylorMade; 60r ©Phil Sheldon; 61bl Ping; 61br Ben Hogan/Callaway Golf; 64tr Ping; 65 Mizuno; 66t & b TaylorMade; 66c Ben Hogan/ Callaway Golf; 67tl & bl Mizuno; 67tr & br Ping; 69 Getty Images/NBAE/Tom Hauck; 70 Mizuno; 72 Ping; 73 Mizuno; 74tr Odyssey/Callaway Golf; 74c & bl Ping; 74l, br & 75t TaylorMade; 75tr & bl Ping; 75cl & cr Mizuno; 75br Odyssey/Callaway Golf; 81t & r Callaway Golf; 82 & 84 Mizuno; 85t Callaway Golf; 85b TaylorMade; 87 Mizuno; 91t Getty Images/AFP/Glynn Kirk; 91b Ping; 93 TaylorMade; 94 Mizuno; 95tl TaylorMade; 95tr Ping; 96r Ping; 96b TaylorMade; 98 © Mikko Pitkänen/Fotolia.com; 102 ProTee United B.V. used with kind permission; 103b Ping; 104 & 105b ©Phil Sheldon; 106 © Laurence Gough/Fotolia. com; 107t © Jan Prchal/Fotolia.com; 107b Corbis/ Sygma/Christina Salvador; 108l ©Phil Sheldon; 109t © Gary Prior/Phil Sheldon; 111b ©Ed Lacey/ Phil Sheldon; 112t © Chad McDermott/Fotolia. com; 112b ©l Stewart/Phil Sheldon; 113 ©Phil Sheldon; 114l ©Phil Sheldon; 114r Top Flite/ Callaway Golf; 115t © H Routledge/Phil Sheldon; 115b Ping; 116 TaylorMade; 118, 119t & br Mizuno; 119 bl Ping; 122 Mizuno; 123bl © D Shopland/Phil Sheldon; 126bl & 128 Ping; 129tr ©Phil Brown/Phil Sheldon; 128bl Mizuno; 130 Getty Images/Scott Halleran; 137t ©Liz Anthony/ Phil Sheldon; 140 © Hobbs Golf Collection; 141r ©Ed Lacey/Phil Sheldon; 144 Mizuno; 146 Birdie Golf Ltd; 147b & 148 ©Phil Sheldon; 149t © Hobbs Golf Collection; 149b Getty Images/Andrew Redington; 150 Getty Images/All Canada Photos/ Henry Georgi; 151b ©Liz Anthony/Phil Sheldon; 152 Corbis/ Macduff Everton; 153t Corbis/Alissa Crandall; 153b Getty Images/Sandra Mu; 154 ©Phil Sheldon; 155b © Hobbs Golf Collection; 158 Mizuno; 160t Ping; 160b & 161 © Hobbs Golf Collection; 163 © Andres Rodriguez/Fotolia. com; 164l TaylorMade; 164r Adidas; 165t TaylorMade; 165c Mizuno; 165bl Ping; 165bl Top Flite/Callaway Golf; 166t & br Ben Hogan/Callaway Golf; 166ct & cl Callaway Golf; 166tl Mizuno; 166tl TaylorMade; 166c Adidas; 166cr & bl Ping; 167 Getty Images/Andrew Redington; 168 ©Liz Anthony/Phil Sheldon; 170t Getty Images/Christian Petersen; 170b TaylorMade; 171tr Top Flite/Callaway Golf; 171l TaylorMade; 171cr Ping; 171br Mizuno; 172tr © J Campion/ Phil Sheldon; 172bl ©Liz Anthony/Phil Sheldon; 175t © J Campion/Phil Sheldon; 176 ©B Greenwood/Phil Sheldon; 177 © H Routledge/Phil Sheldon; 178 ©B Greenwood/Phil Sheldon; 179t © Gary Prior/Phil Sheldon; 179b © J Campion/Phil Sheldon; 181t © J Campion/Phil Sheldon; 181c Mizuno; 181br ©Liz Anthony/Phil Sheldon.

All other photography by Reeve Photography on behalf of Marshall Editions

All other illustrations by Mark Franklin except 69, 78 & 124b by Graham Gaches